Allied Technology Corporation:
An Administrative Assistant Simulation

Donna L. Holmquist
Business Education Program Head
University of Nebraska-Lincoln

Dan B. Holmquist
Internal Graphics and Layout Consultant

JOIN US ON THE INTERNET
WWW: http://www.thomson.com
EMAIL: findit@kiosk.thomson.com   A service of I(T)P®

South-Western Educational Publishing
an International Thomson Publishing company I(T)P®

Team Leader: Karen Schmohe
Developmental Editor: Marilyn Hornsby
Production Coordinator: Jane Congdon
Editor: Denise Wheeler, Carol Spencer
Marketing Manager: Al Roane, Tim Gleim
Art and Design Coordinator: Michelle Kunkler
Cover Design: Creech Creative
Manufacturing Coordinator: Carol Chase
Production Services: Thomas N. Lewis and Teresa M. Boemker

ISBN: 0-538-68131-4
   8 9 10 PR 06 05 04
Printed in the United States of America

Contents

About This Simulation

There are many facets to being an outstanding administrative assistant. Although you will be expected to have most of the necessary skills when you are hired, there are certain procedures that companies want employees to follow so that written and oral communication styles are similar. In the *Company Procedures Manual* you will find reviews of common problem areas in grammar, punctuation, spelling, capitalization, and number and word usage. You will also find specific rules on how records are filed at Allied Technology Corporation.

GENERAL INFORMATION

This simulation represents five days of work during the workweek of January 23 to 27, ——. The work you are expected to do for the week begins on page 65. You are expected to make decisions as to what priority to place on the items and what days to work on the different items. There are some tasks that you will need to work on at different times throughout the week. Your main responsibility is to be sure that all items needed by Mary Andrews are ready for her on the day and at the time she needs them.

This simulation contains specific suggestions from Ms. Andrews as well as general directions for each task. Although you will be working for the manager of the Human Resources and Development Department, you may be doing work for other departments as deemed necessary by Ms. Andrews.

TEMPLATES

Templates have been prepared for specific problems. The templates are available on disk; however, they are not required to perform the problems. You have the option to key problems as you need them.

SUPPLIES

Stationery and other forms used by Allied Technology Corporation can be found at the back of this simulation. In some cases, you may prefer to use the forms that can be found on your template disk.

FOLDERS

You will be required to purchase various folders, labels, and envelopes for use in this simulation. You will need a "Work in Progress" folder to store all unfinished work and a "Completed Work" folder to store copies of completed work. The "Completed Work" folder will be checked by your immediate supervisor (your instructor) at various times throughout the simulation. Each document should be placed in the folder with the heading of the document at the left. The most recent date, or the latest document completed, should be placed in the front of the folder.

ACTIVITY TIME CHARTS

It is important to keep an accurate record of what has been done, what needs to be done, and the time and date of the activity. You will find Activity Time Charts at the back of this simulation. You should be careful to keep accurate records of everything for which you are responsible.

IN-SERVICE ACTIVITIES (QUIZZES)

Every department at Allied Technology Corporation keeps its employees informed and up to date on the latest information and processes. You will have opportunities to improve your skills by completing some of the in-service assignments (quizzes). Your instructor will tell you when each quiz is due.

COPIES

Even though there is talk of a paperless office, it is still not a reality. Allied Technology Corporation requires backup files on the computer as well as a paper copy of each document. All your work should be filed in the correct position in the proper folder (most recent item in front with the top of the article to the left).

DATES

Use the current year as you complete all assignments throughout the simulation.

ACKNOWLEDGMENT

I wish to express my deep appreciation to my husband, Bruce, to my son, Dan, and to my daughters, Teri Wilcox and Amy Jones, for the advice, encouragement, love, and support during the preparation of this project.

Donna Holmquist

Employees' Information Manual

INTRODUCTION TO THE COMPANY

Your name is Chris Downing. You have been hired as an administrative assistant by Allied Technology Corporation (ATC). Allied Technology Corporation has been in business for thirty years and its headquarters is located in Minneapolis, MN. There are six branch offices. You will be working in the Omaha branch office. Information about the headquarters and other branch offices follows.

You report directly to Mary Andrews, manager of the Human Resources and Development Department. You will be successful if you have a clear understanding of the objectives of the business for which you work, and if you are willing to continue learning about new office trends and new kinds of technology.

As an administrative assistant, you must be efficient, knowledgeable, and professional. You must be a decision maker, and you must be willing to change as new methods, ideas, and technology are incorporated into the business. The administrative assistant must work well with all other employees as well as with customers—human relations skills are a necessity. You should be creative as well as intelligent, and you must be able to make quick but good decisions.

The hours of the administrative assistant may vary from day to day. You may be asked to come to work at 7 a.m. instead of 8 a.m., and you may sometimes be asked to stay later than the usual 5 p.m. closing time. Your workload will vary from day to day. A successful administrative assistant has excellent management and organizational skills and tries to identify and plan for rush times in the office.

As a new employee of Allied Technology Corporation, you will begin by studying the *Employees' Information Manual* and the *Company Procedures Manual* so that you are familiar with the structure of the company and the procedures you are expected to follow. In any job situation, it is imperative that you know how to read and follow instructions carefully. For that reason, you should attempt to complete your assignments with as little assistance from the instructor as possible.

HEADQUARTERS INFORMATION

The owner and chief executive officer of Allied Technology Corporation is Henry Simpson. The corporation's main headquarters is located at 4545 State Street, Minneapolis, MN, 55440-0234. The phone number is 612-555-8920. The fax number is 612-555-8930.

BRANCH INFORMATION

Allied Technology Corporation has six branch offices: Omaha, NE; Denver, CO; Los Angeles, CA; Boston, MA; Houston, TX; and Miami, FL. The following table contains information about each branch.

Separate

Branch manager	Branch address, phone, and fax number
Ms. Sally Holiday	Allied Technology Corporation 2323 North Hamilton Avenue Omaha, NE 68144-0111 Phone: 402-555-5555 Fax: 402-555-5444
Mr. Barry Smith	Allied Technology Corporation 6798 North Fremont Street Denver, CO 80218-5544 Phone: 303-555-5341 Fax: 303-555-5342
Ms. Carolyn Lewis	Allied Technology Corporation 2111 Bell Avenue Los Angeles, CA 90012-6776 Phone: 213-555-7878 Fax: 213-555-7834
Mr. Mibu V. Schiavi	Allied Technology Corporation 1823 Hampton Street Boston, MA 02115-3444 Phone: 617-555-0332 Fax: 617-555-0343
Mr. Frank Lake	Allied Technology Corporation 9888 Kennedy Drive Houston, TX 77008-7896 Phone: 713-555-1112 Fax: 713-555-1134
Ms. Deborah Bruckner	Allied Technology Corporation 9290 Regency Parkway Miami, FL 33137-5333 Phone: 305-555-1890 Fax: 305-555-1822

OMAHA OFFICE INFORMATION

Branch manager	Ms. Sally Holiday

Department	Department manager
Accounting	Ms. Cindy Lindley
Legal	Mr. Lee Chung
Marketing	Mr. Jack Bloom
Human Resources and Development	Ms. Mary Andrews
Purchasing	Ms. Charlotte Marks

Separate table

The following is a general description of each department and the educational and/or employment background of each manager.

BRANCH MANAGER

Ms. Sally Holiday is the manager of the Omaha branch. She reports to the Board of Directors regarding the operation of the business. Her job is to communicate the actions of the Board to management and the actions of management to the Board. Ms. Holiday is responsible for visiting other branch offices, speaking at various functions on behalf of the company, and preparing materials for meetings with department managers, other branch managers, and the Omaha area shareholders. She also attends conferences and seminars, and she makes presentations for the company at a multitude of public affairs.

Ms. Holiday's educational background includes a bachelor's degree in Communication and a master's degree in Public Administration.

ACCOUNTING DEPARTMENT

Activities of the Accounting Department include recording all financial transactions; in addition, it involves analyzing, summarizing, and interpreting the financial status of the company and keeping the president apprised of any irregularities. Ms. Cindy Lindley is the manager of this department. Her educational background includes a bachelor's degree in Business Administration and a master's degree in Accounting. She has also passed her Certified Professional Accountant exam and is a CPA.

LEGAL DEPARTMENT

Mr. Lee Chung has been the company's primary lawyer since ATC was founded thirty years ago. He has seen many changes over the years and keeps up to date on legal matters by going to meetings, seminars, and conferences. He must be sure that all items sold in the company are as good as the advertising claims portray them to be. He knows that lawsuits are very prevalent in today's marketplace. He has a staff of attorneys who are available to counsel employees who are involved in lawsuits or other legal problems. Past-due accounts that cannot be collected by the Accounting Department are turned over to this department for processing.

Mr. Chung has a degree in law.

MARKETING DEPARTMENT

Advertising and selling are primary functions for Allied Technology Corporation. Mr. Jack Bloom was a high school marketing teacher before becoming an employee of ATC, and he has had many years of experience in the wholesale and retail markets. He also has a teaching degree in Business Administration with a major in Marketing. His duties include overseeing the sales representatives, spearheading new sales promotions, making decisions regarding new products, setting up trade shows where manufacturers display their products, and arranging sales conferences that are held to motivate and inform the sales personnel regarding new programs and products. He also prepares quarterly and annual reports.

HUMAN RESOURCES AND DEVELOPMENT DEPARTMENT

The Human Resources and Development Department is responsible for announcing job openings, interviewing and testing applicants, and hiring employees. A job description is required for every position. Each employee must have a record on file that shows the date of hire, the salary and benefits offered, a job description, and any other pertinent information. This department also arranges for the best fringe benefits possible for the employees and informs them of any changes in benefits. Any problems that arise within the company may be brought to the manager of this department for consideration and evaluation.

The Human Resources and Development Department also arranges for special appearances of celebrities to promote certain products, plans style shows for memorable occasions, and sends gift items to charity organizations. The department prepares press releases for magazines and newspapers to help advertise the positive aspects of the company. The department also arranges in-service workshops and conferences for company personnel on the latest information and new techniques that pertain to their specific jobs. Recently, the department has also taken responsibility for overseeing the development of physical fitness programs for employees.

Ms. Mary Andrews is the manager of this department. Her educational background consists of a bachelor's

degree in Business Education and a master's degree in Communication.

PURCHASING DEPARTMENT

The manager of the Purchasing Department is Ms. Charlotte Marks. She is responsible for purchasing necessary items for all departments and ensuring that the company stays within its budget each year. Preparation for price lists is disseminated, and each department manager prepares purchase orders for equipment and supplies needed by his/her department. The purchase orders are presented to the Purchasing Department for final approval before anything is purchased. Wholesale items are purchased for resale by the Marketing Department.

Ms. Marks' educational background consists of a bachelor's degree in Business Administration.

Organizational Chart of the Allied Technology Corporation

Create organizational chart

Owner and Chief Executive Officer
Henry Simpson

Branch Managers

Omaha	Denver	Los Angeles	Boston	Houston	Miami
Sally Holiday	Barry Smith	Carolyn Lewis	Mibu V. Schiavi	Frank Lake	Deborah Bruckner

Omaha Office

Branch Manager
Sally Holiday
402-555-5555

Department Managers

Accounting	Legal	Marketing	Human Resources and Development	Purchasing
Cindy Lindley	Lee Chung	Jack Bloom	Mary Andrews	Charlotte Marks
x9090	x8785	x9888	x4445	x7887

Full-Time Employees of the Human Resources and Development Department

Chris Downing	x3352	Mary Pare	x3347
Dwight Harms	x3349	John E. Ross	x3348
Sally Jones	x3324	E.F. Rodriguez	x3350
James Lamberty	x3346	Henry Smythe	x3351

Employee Information for the Human Resources and Development Department

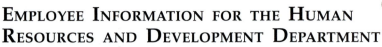 *Employee table Access*

Social Security No.:	603-582-11xx	Name:	Chris Downing
Income Type:	Salary	Address:	13A Clark Road
Monthly Gross Pay:	$1,700		Omaha, NE 68144
Marital Status:	Married	Home Phone:	402-555-9833
Exemptions:	2		
Hired:	9-23-93		
Deductions:			
Life Insurance:	$ 7.95		
Medical Insurance:	$11.34		
Parking:	$10.50		
Savings:	$95.00		

Social Security No.:	503-490-81xx	Name:	Dwight Harms
Income Type:	Salary	Address:	46890 Peach Lane
Monthly Gross Pay:	$1,800		Omaha, NE 68124
Marital Status:	Single	Home Phone:	402-555-4554
Exemptions:	1		
Hired:	10-3-93		
Deductions:			
Life Insurance:	$ 8.95		
Medical Insurance:	$12.34		
Parking:	$ 5.50		
Savings:	$45.00		

Social Security No.:	402-478-88xx	Name:	Sally Jones
Income Type:	Salary	Address:	7531 Sherwood Drive
Monthly Gross Pay:	$1,900		Omaha, NE 68124
Marital Status:	Married	Home Phone:	402-555-6784
Exemptions:	4		
Hired:	7-10-93		
Deductions:			
Life Insurance:	$12.95		
Medical Insurance:	$25.34		
Parking:	$ 5.50		
Savings:	$70.00		

---

add 10 years to hire date

Social Security No.:	502-432-86xx	Name:	James Lamberty
Income Type:	Salary	Address:	1248 Allen Street
Monthly Gross Pay:	$2,700		Omaha, NE 68144
Marital Status:	Married	Home Phone:	402-555-9823
Exemptions:	2		
Hired:	8-20-91		

Deductions:

Life Insurance:	$16.95
Medical Insurance:	$18.34
Dental Insurance:	$ 8.50
Parking:	$12.50
Savings:	$55.00

Social Security No.:	503-352-84xx	Name:	Mary Pare
Income Type:	Salary	Address:	223 Orchard Circle
Monthly Gross Pay:	$2,200		Lincoln, NE 68504
Marital Status:	Single	Home Phone:	402-555-4555
Exemptions:	1		
Hired:	3-6-94 2 wks		

Deductions:

Life Insurance:	$10.50
Medical Insurance:	$15.34
Dental Insurance:	$ 7.00
Parking:	$ 5.50
Savings:	$35.00

Social Security No.:	504-472-33xx	Name:	E.F. Rodriguez
Income Type:	Salary	Address:	5533 Apple Street
Monthly Gross Pay:	$2,700		Papillion, NE 68128
Marital Status:	Married	Home Phone:	402-555-9998
Exemptions:	3		
Hired:	1-9-90		

Deductions:

Life Insurance:	$11.95
Medical Insurance:	$28.34
Parking:	$ 5.50
Savings:	$95.00

Social Security No.:	503-472-88xx	Name:	John E. Ross
Income Type:	Salary	Address:	5678 Allen Street
Monthly Gross Pay:	$2,300		Ralston, NE 68127
Marital Status:	Married	Home Phone:	402-555-1221
Exemptions:	5		
Hired:	5-22-92		
Deductions:			
Life Insurance:	$12.95		
Medical Insurance:	$25.34		
Parking:	$ 5.50		
Savings:	$75.00		

Social Security No.:	603-482-00xx	Name:	Henry Smythe
Income Type:	Salary	Address:	1345A Kelly Road
Monthly Gross Pay:	$2,700		Omaha, NE 68124
Marital Status:	Married	Home Phone:	402-555-3412
Exemptions:	3		
Hired:	4-30-87		
Deductions:			
Life Insurance:	$ 9.95		
Medical Insurance:	$16.34		
Parking:	$10.50		
Savings:	$55.00		

CUSTOMER LIST NO. 34

NAME	ADDRESS	CITY	STATE	ZIP
BETTY J FRANCE	1434 BELL AIRE BLVD	WAHOO	NE	68066
ADELYN LORAN	5784 E SOUTH TEMPLE	SALT LAKE CITY	UT	84102
F C ERICKSON	3589 TEMPLE SQUARE	JOHNSTON	IA	50131
AGNES SMITHSON	2356 OAK DRIVE	RAMIAH	ID	83536
HANNAH SLANDEY	5558 MARINE STREET	SPRING	CA	91360
RUTH JOHN	59 VINTON STREET	OMAHA	NE	68137
B C MEYER	BOX 321	ROSHOLT	SD	57260
REX ALBERTSON	2678 WEST SPRING	NEWCASTLE	WY	82701
MARY KAY SPRIG	15965 METRO	BRONX	NY	10462
ALEX GRIFFIN	4318 GRANT STREET	MINNEAPOLIS	MN	55409
ALLAN ALDRICH	BOX 57	FORT COLLINS	CO	80521
BEVERLY ADAMS	481 NORTH HILLSIDE	BISMARCK	ND	58504
ANDREW JONES	27893 SOUTH 117TH STREET	OMAHA	NE	68144
ANGELA FORNEY	159 DRAKE STREET	OMAHA	NE	68118
ANDREW HANOVER	4444 PRINCETON STREET	BLOOMINGTON	MN	55431-3361
ANNIE MAPERS	78 SUMMERWOOD DRIVE	CHICAGO	IL	60611-5062
SALLY MANE	4598 CHARLOTTE STREET	HOOPER	NE	68031
ANTHONY BUSH	29 S 126TH AVENUE	OMAHA	NE	68107
ARDITH HOWLS	9000 CINDER DRIVE	WAKEFIELD	NE	68784
DELORES JEROMES	BOX 98	FUNK	NE	68940
ALEXANDER BROWN	51 SOUTH PRESIDENTS	FREMONT	NE	68025
JOSEFA S RIOS	2108 16TH AVENUE	GREELEY	CO	80631-5720
TERESA PARKER	4578 ARBOR ROAD	AMES	IA	50010
CAROL BLACK	356 OVERTON DRIVE	ST EDWARD	NE	68660
BRUCE HENDERS	8965 MAPLE STREET	SEWARD	NE	68434-9580
PATRICIA BUCKLEY	6178 JACKSON SQUARE	OMAHA	NE	68137
PENNY SELEE	BOX 34 LOOMIS ROAD	MENLO	GA	30731
RALPH DANNEHY	1225 MARKET STREET	CAMBRIDGE	IL	61238
JANET WILKERS	1301 RIDGEWOOD DRIVE	LINCOLN	NE	68510
DAVID BILLINGSLY	803 S 78TH PLAZA	OMAHA	NE	68152
MARGARET DUNN	3478 HARPER CIRCLE	AXTELL	NE	68924

Access

CUSTOMER LIST NO. 56

COMPANY NAME	ADDRESS	CITY	STATE
LITTLEFIELDS FASHION BOUTIQUE	3125 N 24TH STREET	PHOENIX	AZ
FASHIONS AT LARGE	8544 PARK DRIVE	SPRINGFIELD	IL
MICHAEL'S OF SIOUX FALLS	708 N 120TH STREET	SIOUX FALLS	SD
DANBY OUTLET STORES	3038 N 90TH STREET	COUNCIL BLUFFS	IA
MAURICE'S	120 REGENCY PARKWAY	SCOTTSDALE	AZ
MCGUIRES INC	120 REGENCY CIRCLE	TRENTON	MI
BROOKS FASHIONS	1034 CALIFORNIA STREET	ANNAPOLIS	MD
IRENE'S DRESS SHOP	5002 CENTER STREET	MONTGOMERY	AL
PETITE DISCOVERY	635 N 98TH STREET	KANSAS CITY	KS
BRAGGIE'S	159 REGENCY COURT	LARAMIE	WY
DALTON'S OF SPRINGFIELD	3030 OAKVIEW MALL	SPRINGFIELD	MO
DEB'S SHOP	100 N FORT CROOK ROAD	DETROIT	MI
SEIFERT'S	7201 DODGE STREET	WOODBURY	CT
SURPRISE CLOTHING	5466 N 90TH STREET	DES MOINES	IA
COUNTRY WEAR STORE	7300 WEST DODGE STREET	COSTA MESA	CA
LINCOLN COAT OUTLET	1020 REGENCY CIRCLE	LINCOLN	NE
T S C INDUSTRIES	7910 L STREET	DENVER	CO
MARIO'S OF PALM SPRINGS	3001 S 144TH STREET	SCOTT CITY	KS
BRAUN'S FASHIONS CENTER	7400 DODGE STREET	ALAMEDA	CA
SUITS ME	12103 W CENTER ROAD	WOODSTOCK	TN
FASHION TIME	3445 L STREET	GARDEN CITY	ID
SHE'S A LADY	2511 133RD PLAZA	WOODSBORO	MD
PANJABI'S	5302 S 136TH STREET	FRANKFORT	KY
TAILOR & SONS	360 NORTH SADDLE CREEK	AUSTIN	TX
TAILORED WOMAN	10916 DODGE STREET	WADSWORTH	NV
TALL CONNECTION	2819 PACIFIC STREET	YOUNGSTOWN	NY

Separate table

Company Procedures Manual

AGENDA FORMAT

Allied Technology Corporation Regional Meeting
Board Room No. 24
2323 North Hamilton Avenue
Omaha, NE 68144-0111
January 5, —— 9 a.m.

AGENDA

1. Call to Order .... Sally Holiday

2. Minutes .... Amelia Smith

3. Treasurer's Report .... Robert Meyers

4. Regional Managers' Reports

    Boston .... Mibu V. Schiavi

    Denver .... Barry Smith

    Houston .... Frank Lake

    Los Angeles .... Carolyn Lewis

    Miami .... Deborah Bruckner

    Omaha .... Sally Holiday

5. Convention Report .... Billie Sheele

6. Legislative Action Report .... Jerry Coxen

7. Program of Work .... Sally Holiday

8. Public Relations Committee .... Martha Young

9. Budget Discussion .... Robert Meyers

10. Old Business .... Sally Holiday

11. New Business .... Sally Holiday

12. Adjournment .... Sally Holiday

APPOINTMENT SCHEDULING

- Discuss with the employer the best times for appointments to be made.
- Discuss with the employer the guidelines concerning interruptions. (In case of an emergency interruption, write the message on a piece of paper and hand it to your employer.)
- Avoid overscheduling appointments on Monday or after the employer has been out of town.
- Avoid overscheduling appointments when the employer is preparing for a trip.
- Place applicable files and documents in employer's office to allow him/her to prepare for an appointment.
- Place extra chairs in the employer's office if extra visitors are expected.
- Plan to offer beverages if that is the acceptable custom in your office.
- Inform reception area of expected visitors and initiate security clearances if required.
- Arrange for special services if visitor is disabled.
- Provide unscheduled time between appointments in case an appointment takes longer than expected.
- Make outside-the-office appointments at convenient times for the employer.
- Allow the employer time to process the mail.
- Keep a record of office visitors—date, time, purpose of visit.

CAPITALIZATION RULES*

(*SEE A REFERENCE GUIDE FOR ADDITIONAL RULES)

Titles of people or positions. Capitalize titles when they precede a name. Do not capitalize titles when they follow a name unless they refer to high government officials. (This rule does not apply to the envelope or inside address.)

- We were greeted by Professor Robinson.
- It was forwarded to Chairman Brown.
- We were greeted by Lloyd Robbins, professor of English.
- It was forwarded to Mr. Henry Cooper, chairman of the committee.
- Mrs. Neil McElroy, Secretary of the Interior, will be our speaker.
- Mrs. Mary Nolan, secretary-treasurer of the organization, will take up the collection.

Specific and general classifications. Capitalize the names of specific departments, but do not capitalize the names of general classifications.

- The Human Resources and Development Department administers employment tests.
- Most employment offices are very busy places today.

Directions such as north, south, east, west. When certain sections of the country are specified by directions, they should be capitalized. When the directions are general, they should not be capitalized.

- We will be going to Southern California next summer.
- Nebraska is a part of the Middle West region.
- They live east of Chicago.
- We will be traveling west into the sun.

Words in headings and titles. Capitalize the word *the* when it is the first word of a title. Capitalize the important words in headings and titles, such as nouns, pronouns, verbs, adverbs, and adjectives. Minor words are not capitalized, such as prepositions (*of, in, to, by*), conjunctions (*and, but, or*), articles (*a, an, the*), and often small verbs (*is, are, be*).

- <u>The Battle of the Marne</u> is a good book to read.
- <u>How to Write a Short Story</u> should be helpful for this class.

CERTIFICATE FORMAT

The following is a model of a certificate form often used at Allied Technology Corporation.

Here let it be known that

_____

has satisfactorily completed
the workshop

_____

_____   _____
Instructor   **Date**

ENVELOPE INFORMATION

- There are two sizes of envelopes: No. 6, which is 6 1/2 inches by 3 5/8 inches; and No. 10, which is 9 1/2 inches by 4 1/8 inches.

- Use No. 6 envelopes for a one-page letter or memorandum. Use No. 10 envelopes for a one-page letter or memorandum with enclosures or for a two-page letter or memorandum.

- If an item is bulky or cannot be folded, use a manila envelope, which may be 9 inches by 12 inches or 10 inches by 13 inches.

- The return address is the preprinted company address—key the sender's name or department name or number above the return address to expedite handling if it is returned.

- AIRMAIL, CERTIFIED MAIL, REGISTERED MAIL, PRIORITY MAIL, RETURN RECEIPT REQUESTED, and SPECIAL DELIVERY notations should be placed in all capital letters in the upper right corner of the envelope below the postage area.

- ATTENTION, CONFIDENTIAL, HOLD FOR ARRIVAL, PERSONAL, and PLEASE FORWARD are special instructions that should be placed in all capital letters in the upper left corner of the envelope below the return address.

- All words in an address should be spelled in full, except the two-letter state abbreviation and other accepted abbreviations requested by the post office for more efficient use with the Optical Character Reader (OCR).

- Refer to a secretarial handbook for proper ways to address different dignitaries, such as Reverend, Senator, Representative, President, etc.

- Call the post office for rate schedules and specific mailing information (or check with the company postal division).

- For interoffice mail, use a company envelope. Key the recipient's name in all caps approximately 13 lines from the top at the approximate center of the envelope. On the next line, key the department name (if you know it).

- When keying the name and address of the recipient, follow these postal guidelines:

  1. Use single spacing and a block format.
  2. Begin keying the address at the horizontal and vertical center of the envelope.
  3. Key the city, state, and ZIP Code as the last line of the address.
  4. Do not place any information below or to the side of the address block.
  5. Use a simple block typeface. Do not use script or italic type.
  6. *Always* include a return address.
  7. The address should be in all capital letters in a 10, 12, or 14 point sans serif font, without punctuation.
  8. Use the two-letter state abbreviations.
  9. If you know the entire ZIP+4 code, its use will speed the delivery of your mail.
  10. A computer barcode is placed in the lower right-hand corner during processing. Barcodes may also be applied by the customer using special word processing packages or addressing machines.

FAX Cover Sheet Format

FAX COVER SHEET

DATE:

TO:

FAX NUMBER:

FROM:

**NUMBER OF PAGES
INCLUDING THIS
COVER SHEET:**

MESSAGE:

**If any part of this fax
transmission is missing
or not clearly received,
please call:**

NAME:

PHONE NUMBER:

FILING GUIDELINES

- File every day—all filing must be kept up to date.
- File at a slow time of day when interruptions are few—file at the same time each day to make sure the filing gets done.
- Arrange unfiled records in a sorter so that you can find a record quickly when it is requested.
- Prior to going to the file drawer, place items in alphabetical order so they are ready to be put into the file folders when you get to the file drawers.
- Arrange records in chronological order within the folder with the most recent date at the front of the folder.
- Place all items in the folders in the same fashion—with the top of the document at the left of the folder.
- If you spend a great deal of time trying to find items in the files, you may need to add more guides.
- Once a folder has about three-fourths of an inch of material, it is time to add another folder.
- Leave three to four inches of working space in every file drawer.
- Always close a file drawer before opening the next drawer—if you have two drawers open at once, the file cabinet may tip over.
- When a record is removed from the file, put something in its place—an "out" sheet or a slip of colored paper—noting what was taken, when, and by whom.
- Keep folder tabs readable and in good condition, replace broken guides, and use quality folders that do not sag.
- Maintain an index of folder captions when using a subject file so that duplication will not occur.
- Keep a record of who has checked out a folder so you can follow up on it if it is not returned within a reasonable amount of time.
- Have files and records returned to an in-basket on your desk.
- Permit only designated personnel to use the files—refile most of the folders yourself.
- Transfer old files to a permanent storage location or microfilm certain records.
- Develop a filing manual and insist on its use.

FINDING LOST RECORDS

- Check the folders before and after the one where the record belongs; check between the folders and at the bottom of the drawer.
- Look for a similar name or number. Look under other vowels following the initial letter.
- See if the name or number was transposed.
- Check alternative letters and spellings.
- Try a similar-sounding spelling.
- Check to see if the item could be en route.
- Check the in-basket on the administrative assistant's desk and on the boss's desk.
- Check the miscellaneous folder to see if a special name folder should have been used.
- Contact the last person who used the folder or item.
- Look in the relative index for titles under which the material might have been filed.

INTEROFFICE MEMORANDUM FORMAT

A
T
C

INTEROFFICE MEMORANDUM

To: Employees of Allied Technology Corporation
From: Mary Andrews *MA*
Date: Current Date
Subject: Interoffice Memorandum Format

This is an example of the interoffice memorandum format used at Allied Technology Corporation. It should be keyed into your computer so that all you need to do is retrieve the file and enter the correct information.

Titles are not used in the To and From lines. Leave two blank lines before keying the body of the memorandum.

Single space the body of the memorandum and double space between paragraphs. Paragraphs may be block or indented format. If enumerated items are used, single space the items at the left margin and leave one blank line between the items.

Use 1-inch side margins. Most memorandums are short and may be keyed on half-size paper (5 1/2 inches long). If the memorandum is longer than one page, use the same style header that is used on the second page of a letter (see page 56 of this manual).

After the last line of the body of the memorandum, leave one blank line before each of the following notations: the typist's initials, attachment (if applicable), and copy (copies).

The person sending the memorandum should place his/her initials after the keyed name in the From line to indicate that the message is ready to be distributed in the company mail.

A memorandum does not usually need an envelope unless the information is private. The envelope should have the keyed name and office address (all caps) of the person to whom it is being sent.

cd

Attachment

c Department Managers
   Support Staff

ITINERARY FORMAT

An itinerary (see page 26) is a travel plan that provides all information on where a person will be, with exact dates and times. It also gives information about the travel and lodging accommodations; the people to meet (and where and when); any necessary phone numbers and addresses; and meeting locations, times, and attendees. Begin the itinerary 2 inches from the top of the page. Make three copies—one for the office and two for the individual (one for his/her use and one that can be left at his/her home).

JOB DESCRIPTION FOR ADMINISTRATIVE ASSISTANT

Each branch manager has an administrative assistant who is responsible for carrying out the activities of that particular branch office. The administrative assistant may have several employees who report to him/her; however, the administrative assistant is responsible for seeing that the office runs smoothly and that all tasks are completed on time. Following is a list of the responsibilities and characteristics of the administrative assistant:

- Processes incoming mail
- Composes correspondence and reports
- Maintains composure during stressful periods
- Exercises decision-making skills
- Completes myriad administrative duties
- Researches and abstracts information
- Maintains a records management system within the office
- Coordinates conferences, meetings, and executive travel
- Supervises clerical employees
- Schedules appointments and maintains a calendar
- Keys documents
- Organizes time and tasks
- Transcribes from notes or tapes
- Acts as public relations person for his/her boss and the company
- Evaluates personnel working for him/her
- Processes telephone calls
- Exercises effective human relations

ITINERARY FOR JACK BLOOM
Omaha, NE to Denver, CO
May 12-13, ——

TUESDAY, MAY 12: DEPART FROM OMAHA TO DENVER

6:00 a.m.   Check on plane departure time (Interstate Airlines Flight 204 to Denver--555-9992). Call taxi--555-5647.

7:00 a.m.   Taxi to airport.

8:30 a.m.   Depart Interstate Airlines Flight 204 to Denver. Reserved seat 5A.

8:25 a.m.   Arrive at Denver airport. Take hotel limousine to Villa Hotel at
(Denver time)   1665 Adams Street. Suite confirmation No. 43345. Phone No. 303-555-4444.

11:30 a.m.   Luncheon meeting in Columbia Room of the Villa. Bring drafts of the revised marketing plan. Others attending meeting: Shirley Henry, Los Angeles; Peter Bogs, Miami; and Herman Holt, Denver. Arrangements have been made for the luncheon and use of the room until 5:30 p.m.

7:00 p.m.   Taxi to "Evening Out Club" at 1414 Hillsdale Avenue for dinner with Barry Smith from the Denver branch office. All arrangements have been made for party of two. Phone No. 303-555-9090.

WEDNESDAY, MAY 13: RETURN TO OMAHA

9:00 a.m.   Continuation of meeting in Columbia Room of the Villa with Henry, Bogs, and Holt. Luncheon arrangements have been made with the hotel. Check out of hotel before noon. Check bags.

5:30 p.m.   Close meeting. Check on plane departure time (Interstate Flight No. 898 to Omaha--Phone No. 303-555-9992).

6:00 p.m.   Hotel limousine to airport.

7:30 p.m.   Depart Interstate Airlines Flight 898 to Omaha. Reserved seat 7A. Dinner on plane.

9:35 p.m.   Arrive at Omaha airport. Take taxi to home.
(Omaha time)

LETTER FORMAT (BLOCK)

Allied
Technology
Corporation

1   2323 North Hamilton Avenue • Omaha, NE 68144-0111
(402) 555-5555 • Fax (402) 555-5444 • E-mail hfm@aolemc.com

2 Current Date   (Space may be adjusted here to allow for different letter lengths.)

3 Atlantic Supply Company
4565 Marble Street
Miami, FL 33101-7986

4 Ladies and Gentlemen   (Refer to page 54 of this manual for examples of other salutations.)

5 Directions for block letter style: All lines begin at the left margin and there are no tabulator stops for indentations. Open punctuation is more efficient. Margins vary according to the length of a letter: 1 inch, long letter; 1 1/2 inches, medium letter; 2 inches, short letter. Use single spacing unless letter is very short.

The company name may be keyed in all caps and placed two spaces below the complimentary close. (This is most often used for letters going out-of-house.) Only the initials of the person who keyed the document are placed on the line two spaces below the signature line. (If the letter was dictated by someone other than the person whose name is keyed on the signature line, that person's initials are placed in front of the typist's initials.) Use a single "c" for copy or "pc" for photocopy ("cc" represented "carbon copy" and is no longer relevant) followed by name(s) of people to whom copies of the letter will be sent. Leave a uniform margin of 6 to 12 lines at the bottom of each page (except the last page, which may run short).

Letters with two or more pages require a heading at the top of the second page as shown on page 56 of this manual. Use plain paper. Carry over at least two lines of the letter, plus the closing.

6 Sincerely yours

7 ALLIED TECHNOLOGY CORPORATION

(Space may be adjusted here to allow for different letter lengths.)

8 Ms. Sally Holiday
Manager

9 cd   (Nos. 9, 10, and 11 should be keyed with double spaces between them.)

10 Enclosure

11 c Ms. Millie Burke
Mr. Adrian Romero

1—Letterhead, 2—Dateline, 3—Inside Address, 4—Salutation, 5—Body, 6—Complimentary Close, 7—Organization Name, 8—Writer and Title (Signature Line), 9—Reference Initials, 10—Enclosure Notation, 11—Copy Notation

LETTER FORMAT (SIMPLIFIED)

*A*llied
*T*echnology
*C*orporation

2323 North Hamilton Avenue • Omaha, NE 68144-0111
1   (402) 555-5555 • Fax (402) 555-5444 • E-mail hfm@aolemc.com

2 Current Date   **(Space may be adjusted here to allow for different letter lengths.)**

3 Atlantic Supply Company
4565 Marble Street
Miami, FL 33101-7986

4 THE SIMPLIFIED LETTER STYLE

5 The simplified letter style is keyed in block style with all lines beginning at the left margin. The salutation is replaced by a subject line keyed in all capital letters. This is placed two blank lines below the inside address. Two blank lines separate the subject line from the body of the letter.

The complimentary close is omitted and the writer's name and title are keyed three or four blank lines below the body of the letter. Use all capital letters.

Letters with two or more pages require a heading at the top of the second page as shown on page 56 of this manual. Use plain paper. Carry over at least two lines of the letter, plus the closing.

6 SALLY HOLIDAY, MANAGER   **(Space may be adjusted here to allow for different letter lengths.)**

7 cd

8 Enclosure   **(Nos. 7, 8, and 9 should be keyed with double spaces between them.)**

9 c Ms. Millie Burke
       Mr. Adrian Romero

1—Letterhead, 2—Dateline, 3—Inside Address, 4—Subject Line, 5—Body, 6—Writer and Title (Signature Line), 7—Reference Initials, 8—Enclosure Notation, 9—Copy Notation

MEETING PREPARATIONS

Committee Meetings

- In general, these meetings are held on the company premises and usually relate to normal business activity.
- Select a time and date convenient for all committee members.
- Send a reminder of the meeting—ask for items for the agenda.
- Prior to each meeting, provide the chairperson with an agenda or list of topics to be discussed during the order of business—these usually include the call to order, announcements, introductions of new members or guests, reports of standing committees, old business, new business, and adjournment.
- Send an agenda to all committee members and to any others invited to the meeting.
- Prepare the room—temperature, water glasses, seating arrangements, equipment.
- Prepare a membership roster and call the roll when required.
- Keep an accurate record of the activities of each meeting by recording and keying minutes.
- When called upon, read back the exact wording of a motion that is before the group.
- Verify the accuracy of the minutes by signature.
- Read papers, correspondence, etc., that may be called for by the group.
- Furnish information from minutes as requested by other officers or members.
- Keep records, reports, and other documents not assigned to other officers.
- Provide the chairperson of a committee with copies of reports, papers, correspondence, etc., that are applicable to that committee's work.
- When called upon, provide a copy of the organization's constitution and by-laws, rules, list of membership, list of committees, etc.
- At the end of the meeting, put the room back in order.
- If the meeting is to be a luncheon or dinner meeting, make arrangements for food service.
- After the meeting, key the minutes and distribute them to all committee members as soon as possible. (Refer to the format on pages 31–32 of this manual.)
- Make a special note of any items that you are responsible for completing.

Conventions

- Obtain a list of hotels and their facilities from the convention bureau in the city where the convention will be held.
- See that dates, times, places, and other pertinent information regarding the convention is sent to prospective attendees early enough so that they can make suitable arrangements to attend—include information such as distance from airport, cost of transportation services, etc.
- Find out from the speakers what their audio-visual or other equipment requirements will be.
- Assemble all printed information, oversee the keying of the final copy of the program, work with the professional printer for final copy corrections, etc.
- Make arrangements for a registration desk in the lobby of the hotel and for people to work at the registration desk.
- During the convention, check on arrangements and be available to answer questions and handle problems as they arise.

Minutes Format

Allied Technology Corporation
Executive Board Minutes
January 5, ——
Omaha Branch Office

CALL TO ORDER	The meeting of the Executive Board of Allied Technology Corporation was held at the Omaha branch office on Thursday, January 5, ——. Sally Holiday called the meeting to order at 9 a.m.
ROLL CALL	The administrative assistant, Amelia Smith, called the roll. The following individuals were present: Deborah Bruckner, Jerry Coxen, Sally Holiday, Frank Lake, Carolyn Lewis, Robert Meyers, Mibu V. Schiavi, Billie Sheele, Amelia Smith, Barry Smith, Martha Young.
MINUTES	Amelia Smith read the minutes from the last meeting. There were no changes to the minutes.
TREASURER'S REPORT	Robert Meyers gave the treasurer's report. A copy of the report is attached.
REGIONAL MANAGERS' REPORTS	The managers from the Boston, Denver, Houston, Los Angeles, Miami, and Omaha regions presented their reports of activities since the last meeting. The reports are attached.
CONVENTION REPORT	Billie Sheele reported that the plans for the coming convention are on schedule. She gave a brief explanation of some of the topics that will be covered and the speakers whom she has contacted.
LEGISLATIVE ACTION COMMITTEE REPORT	Jerry Coxen reported that he was pleased with the response to his request for volunteers to assist him with this committee. He now has ten assistants.
PROGRAM OF WORK DISCUSSION	The program of work was presented by Sally Holiday. There was considerable discussion about the need to revise hiring standards and the plan to reduce personnel. This item was tabled for further discussion at the next meeting.

PUBLIC RELATIONS COMMITTEE	Martha Young indicated that the Public Relations Committee has been working hard and has come up with some excellent suggestions for improving the public relations of our organization. These will be reported on in detail at the next meeting.
BUDGET DISCUSSION	Robert Meyers asked that the regional managers carefully examine their budget needs for the next six months and let him know what their projections are. He indicated that funds are tight and that each region needs to trim expenses as much as possible.
OLD BUSINESS	None
NEW BUSINESS	There will be a seminar on August 25 in Dallas for promotion of special products. More information will be sent to each manager soon.
NEXT MEETING	The next meeting will be held on Thursday, February 2, at the Denver branch office.
ADJOURNMENT	Sally Holiday adjourned the meeting at 12:40 p.m.

_____

(Signature of Administrative Assistant)

Attachments: Treasurer's Report
Regional Managers' Reports

NUMBER RULES

Spelling vs. using figures. In general, spell out numbers up to and including *ten*. Use figures above *ten*. Indefinite or approximate numbers are spelled out.

- 11 women
- ten video tapes
- about seventy-five people

Spell numbers in full at the beginning of a sentence, even when figures are used later in the sentence. (If possible, try to rewrite the sentence so that it does not start with a number.)

- Seventy-six women went to the rally.
- There were 76 women at the rally.

If several numbers are used in a sentence, key all numbers as figures.

- Please order 6 sets of pencils, 20 packages of computer paper, and 112 boxes of staples.

Spelled out compound numbers below 100 should be hyphenated.

- We are waiting for sixty-five reams of paper.

Percentages. Use figures and the word *percent* to express percentages.

- 5 percent

Physical measures. Express dimensions, weights, and distance in figures.

- The room is 8" x 10".
- The cat weighs 9 pounds.
- Miriam hiked 16 miles yesterday.

Money. Use figures for amounts of money. Express even sums of money without the decimal and ciphers. Use figures and the word *cents* to express amounts under $1.

- $345.70
- $90
- 30 cents

Time. Use a figure with the abbreviations *a.m.* and *p.m.* and with the word *o'clock*. Spell out the hour when it is expressed in an informal way.

- The office opens at 8:15 a.m.
- The office closes at 5 p.m.

- The office closes at 5 o'clock.
- I leave at five-thirty in the evening.

Dates. After the name of the month, use figures to express the day. Use *d*, *st*, or *th* when the day of the month stands alone or when it precedes the month.

- March 20
- We will go to Alaska on the 21st of next month.
- On the 28th of February, we will celebrate his birthday.

Age. Spell out years of age, but use figures to express ages or periods of time given in a combination of years, months, and days.

- He is twenty years old.
- Grandpa is 60 years, 6 months, and 20 days old.

Invoice terms. Use figures to express invoice terms.

- A discount of 5%, 15 days, is allowed.

Ordinal numbers. Spell out ordinal numbers ending with the sounds *st*, *nd*, *rd*, and *th*, except when they are part of a date or street address. *First* and *second* are examples of ordinal numbers.

- The twentieth century was a time of extensive changes.
- We celebrated our third wedding anniversary last year.
- This is the first time we will be able to leave this country safely.

Isolated figures. Spell out isolated figures except when doing so would be awkward.

Addresses. Spell out the numbered names of streets and avenues up to and including *ten*.

- 125 West Tenth Street
- 535 East 80th Street

Use figures to express all room, apartment, and post office box numbers and all house numbers except the number *one*.

- Room 3490
- One Chestnut Drive
- 2 Apple Street

Other figures. Use figures to express page numbers and numbers that identify invoice orders, insurance policies, and bank or credit accounts.

- Page 3489
- Your account number is 4367.

OUTLINE FORMAT

Use periods after letters and numbers in alphanumeric outlines, except those set off by parentheses. Leave two blank spaces before beginning the contents of the item. In topic outlines, the only other punctuation is after abbreviations. In sentence outlines, appropriate end-of-line punctuation is used.

Every level of division must have at least two elements: If there is an A, there must be a B. If there is a 1, there must be a 2, etc. Main headings (I, II, etc.) may be keyed in all caps with double spacing above and below them. Other patterns of spacing may be used as long as they are consistent throughout the outline. For all remaining lines of a topic outline, capitalize only the first letter of important words. In sentence outlines, capitalize the first letter of the first word of the sentence, and other words as appropriate.

ALPHANUMERIC OUTLINE—EXAMPLE 1

(NOTE: NOT ALL LEVELS WILL BE NECESSARY FOR EVERY OUTLINE)

```
I.   xxxx
     A.   xxxx
     B.   xxxx
          1.   xxxx
          2.   xxxx
               a.   xxxx
               b.   xxxx
                    (1)   xxxx
                    (2)   xxxx
                          (a)   xxxx
                          (b)   xxxx
                                1)   xxxx
                                2)   xxxx
                                     a)   xxxx
                                     b)   xxxx
     C.   xxxx
     D.   xxxx

II.  xxxx
```

ALPHANUMERIC OUTLINE—EXAMPLE 2

```
I.   First Major Topic
     A.   A section of the first major topic
          1.   The first subdivision of section A
               a.   Part of 1, above
               b.   Another part of 1, above
          2.   The second subdivision of section A

II.  Second Major Topic
     A.   A section of the second major topic
     B.   Another section of the second major
          topic
```

PARLIAMENTARY TERMS

Adjourn. To end a meeting officially

Adjourned meeting. A continuation of a regular or special meeting held at another time

Adopt. To approve

Agenda. A list of official business to be covered at a meeting

Amend. To change

Ballot. A paper or mechanical device used to record votes privately

Bylaw. A rule of an organization

Carried. Approved by the required number of votes

Chair. The presiding officer

Constitution. Fundamental laws and principles of government adopted by an organization

Convene. To open a meeting formally

Debate. A discussion on a matter before the group

Disappearing quorum. The required number of persons were present at the beginning of the meeting, but not at the end of the meeting

Discussion. A debate or oral presentation of viewpoints by different people

General consent. The same as unanimous consent; an informal method of disposing of routine business by the presiding officer assuming the group's approval

Main motion. A motion presented to a group for consideration

Majority vote. More than half of the number legally voting

Minority vote. Less than half of the number legally voting

Minutes. The official record of actions taken by an organization

Motion. A proposal, usually introduced by the words "I move," that is submitted to a group for consideration

New business. Business other than what was old or unfinished from a previous meeting

Nomination. A formal proposal of a person for an office

Order of business. The sequence of items of business to be considered at the meeting

Out of order. Not in keeping with accepted parliamentary procedure at a particular time

Parliamentarian. A person skilled in parliamentary procedure

Postpone definitely. To put off consideration of a motion or report until a specific time

Postpone indefinitely. To cancel a motion or report so it will not be considered at any time

Preamble. An introduction to a constitution or resolution stating its purpose

Precedence. Order of priority or rank

Presiding officer. The person who conducts a meeting

Proxy. A signed statement transferring one's right to vote to another person

Quorum. The number of members who must be present to conduct business legally

Roll call. A call of members in a fixed order

Second. Approval of a proposed motion for consideration by the group

Special meeting. A meeting called to consider special business

Standing committee. A committee set up to handle all business related to a certain subject

Teller. Member who assists in conducting voting by ballot

PAYROLL PROCESSING

Employee Income Classifications

Salaried Employee. A salaried employee earns a fixed amount of money each week or month. The salaried positions are usually held by higher-level or management employees. A salaried employee earns the same amount of money each week no matter how many hours he or she works.

Hourly Employee. An hourly employee earns a set rate of money per hour for each hour worked. Forty hours per week is considered a normal workweek for an hourly employee. Hours that are worked beyond 40 hours per week are considered to be overtime. Employees are usually paid a bonus for the overtime hours worked. Allied Technology Corporation pays time-and-a-half for overtime hours, which is equal to one-and-a-half times the employee's regular hourly rate. If an hourly employee's regular rate is $8 an hour, the overtime rate would be $12 an hour.

Commissioned Employee. A commissioned employee earns a percentage of the total merchandise he or she sells. Salespeople are often paid on a commission basis, which is an incentive for them to maintain a high sales volume. As the salespeople earn more for the business, they also earn more for themselves. Salespeople at Allied Technology Corporation earn a 5 percent commission on their sales. If a commissioned employee sells $20,000 of goods in one week, for example, that person earns $1,000 for that week.

Payroll Deductions

Federal Income Tax. The amount of federal income tax withheld for payment to the federal government depends upon the employee's gross pay, marital status, and the number of exemptions claimed. An exemption is an allowance that permits employees to reduce their tax payments if they are responsible for paying more than half of the support of a spouse, children, or other adults. Each employee reports the number of exemptions he/she claims on an *Employee's Withholding Allowance Certificate* form, known as the W-4 form. The amount of money withheld for federal income tax decreases as the number of exemptions increases.

Federal Insurance Contributions Act (FICA) Tax. An employee's annual gross pay is taxed to support the federal social security system. The employer is required to match the amount of money withheld for each employee. The percent of gross pay withheld for FICA tax changes from year to year.

State Income Tax. State income tax must be paid on all income earned within the state; this applies to residents and nonresidents of the state. Tax rates vary among the states—some have fixed percentages for all employees while others are based on number of exemptions claimed and on marital status.

Voluntary Payroll Deductions. Employees may request to have money withheld from their paychecks for such things as life insurance, medical insurance, dental insurance, pension plans, parking privileges, and savings plans.

Payroll Register. At Allied Technology Corporation, each employee receives a payroll register form along with his/her weekly or monthly paycheck. The form itemizes the year-to-date cumulative totals for gross and net pay, federal and state income taxes, FICA tax, health and life insurance, savings plans, and other deductions.

PROOFREADING SUCCESSFULLY

Even though most office workers have spell checkers on their word processing programs, letters containing proofreading errors are still received and sent. Here are some common proofreading aids to help eliminate errors from items prepared at the Allied Technology Corporation.

- Speed reading is out when you are proofreading! You need to concentrate on the words and the meaning of the keyed material.
- Proofread and, if possible, wait until tomorrow to proofread again, or have someone else proofread it for you.

- Pay attention to dates, especially when a new year has arrived.
- Do not overlook the name, address, subject or reference line, signature line, or copy notation. Be sure names and addresses are spelled correctly.
- Read through difficult material backward to check for spelling errors.
- Check a reference manual to be sure about hyphenating a word.
- Read the body of the letter carefully to be sure that words such as *or*, *that*, and *the* haven't been missed, slipped in unexpectedly, or perhaps been repeated.
- Proofread in steps: check all headings and titles first, then see if page numbers are correct and in sequence.
- Be sure that references to specific page numbers are correct and that the material is actually on the page number referred to.
- If there are footnotes, check to be sure that they have been keyed correctly and that the information is accurate. This may require you to look at the original reference.
- When verifying data, it is a good idea for two people to double-check figures. Do this by having one person read the numbers aloud to the other person.
- Place a ruler below the lines as you read them—this will help you keep your place and, if you are interrupted, you will be able to resume at the place you left off.
- Outlines can be checked by breaking them into parts—check headings, numbers, letters, indentations, and the written material.
- When keying columns, check the number of entries on the original and compare it to the new keyed copy to see if you have omitted anything.
- Watch for deletions of *ed* or *s* on your words.
- Be consistent in the use of commas. If you must read a sentence more than once to understand the meaning, you may need to add or delete a comma.
- If possible, have someone else read your material to see if it is accurate.
- Even though you have a spell checker, it cannot make judgments between words such as *their* and *there*, *hear* and *here*, or *to*, *too*, and *two*.
- Be consistent in the use of capital letters. Refer to a reference manual if you are in doubt about what is correct.

Proofreader's Marks

add a space	#	This is the correct way to mark a sentence where a space should be added.
new paragraph	¶	¶ This sentence should start a new paragraph.
delete, take out	ℓ	The letter "e" needs to be deleted from the word "be."
let it stand as it was	*stet*	Here is the correct way to undo a correction that should be changed.
change a letter	/	Please come tomorrow.
close up	⌣	Some times a word needs to be closed so that there is no space in it.
transpose copy	∿	Typists often transpsoe letters and words even.
insert	∧	It is easy to miss letter or word occasionally.
move right	⌐	This sentence is out of alignment with the others.
move left	⌐	This sentence is out of alignment with the others.
use capital letters	≡	The book is titled Take it Easy.
use lowercase	/ lc	It was the nicest day we had all Winter.
single space	*ss*	We were going to the park when the fire engine roared past us. We decided to follow it although we knew that was not recommended.
double space	*ds*	Soon we saw the police cars and several ambulances. It was scary to see all that equipment so close to our home. Were they at our house?
use a period	⊙	Mr. Johnson and Miss Smith will be serving the dinner.
spell out	*sp*	The Rev. Jones will give the closing prayer.
underscore	⎯	The noise was very loud!
move	⌣↗	evening
bold	∿∿	I was so happy!
center	][	] Chapter 3 [

PUNCTUATION RULES

Parenthetical Comments. A writer sometimes inserts a comment or an explanation that could be omitted without changing the meaning of the sentence. Such added comments and explanations are called *parenthetical* and are separated from the rest of the sentence by commas.

If the parenthetical word or phrase occurs at the beginning or end of a sentence, only one comma is needed.

- I think, therefore, that we will go to the mall anyway.
- Don't you think, Miss Smith, that the temperature is too cold?
- We shall send you the book, of course.

Apposition. A writer sometimes mentions a person or thing and then, in order to make the meaning perfectly clear to the reader, he/she says the same thing again in different words. An expression in apposition is set off by two commas, except at the end of a sentence, when only one comma is necessary.

- My friend, Ricardo Torres, flies his own plane.
- The meeting will be held on Saturday, January 23, at the University Square.
- We will meet you on Saturday, March 30.

Series. When the last item in a series of three or more is preceded by *and*, *or*, or *nor*, place a comma before the conjunction, as well as between the other items.

- He bought pencils, paper, and glue at the store.
- I will be out of town on May 3, June 6, and August 23.
- She will key the letters, enclose the brochures, and address the envelopes.

Dependent Clause. When a sentence starts with a dependent clause, it requires another clause to complete the thought. Such clauses are called *dependent* or *subordinate* clauses. Dependent clauses begin with such words as *after, although, as, because, before, if, now, when, whenever, where, whether, while, until,* and *unless.* Use a comma to separate the two clauses.

- As I told you on the phone, we will be at your home for dinner.
- When I receive the check in the mail, I will let you know immediately.
- If you cannot come to the meeting, please let me know.
- While I would rather not hear about it, it will probably be on all the news stations.
- Unless I hear from you soon, I will not be going to the conference.

Introductory Words and Phrases. Introductory words or phrases include the following: *furthermore*, *for instance*, and *incidentally*. These words or phrases are followed by a comma.

- For instance, the abbreviation NB is often used for Nebraska instead of NE.
- Furthermore, I really didn't want to talk to him.
- Incidentally, neither of us liked the book.

Independent Clause. An independent clause has a subject and a predicate and can stand alone as a complete sentence. When two independent clauses are closely related, they are often connected with a coordinating conjunction such as *and, but, or, for,* or *nor.* When two independent clauses are connected with a coordinating conjunction, a comma is used before the conjunction.

- We will go to the sale on Tuesday, and I plan to go to another sale on Friday.
- The microwave is the most efficient on the market, and it is also the least expensive.

With Semicolon. When a comma occurs within one or both independent clauses in a sentence, place a semicolon between the two independent clauses.

- Our sales receipt shows, Miss Burns, that you received the item on sale; we will be happy to refund the sale price to you.

With No Conjunction. When two independent clauses are closely related but no conjunction connects them, use a semicolon. The sentences could also be written as two separate sentences with a period in place of the semicolon.

- Mable received five awards for her activities; Betty received three awards.

And Omitted. When two or more adjectives modify the same noun, they are separated by commas. However, do not use a comma if the first adjective modifies the combined idea of the second adjective plus the noun.

- He has a silly, colorful outfit.
- She will be a quiet, helpful resource.
- He has a blue silk tie.
- Mary has large brown eyes.

Note: It is easy to determine whether to insert a comma between two consecutive adjectives by mentally placing *and* between them. If the sentence makes sense with *and* inserted between the adjectives, then the comma is used. The first two sentences would read as follows: He has a silly *and* colorful outfit. She will be a quiet *and* helpful resource.

Omission Commas.   Use commas to show the omission of words within the sentence.

- Mr. Strong will arrive tomorrow; Mr. Armor, on Friday.

Illustrative Material.   When an illustration is introduced by an expression such as *namely, specifically, that is,* or *for example,* the expression is preceded by a semicolon and followed by a comma.

- We would like this room to be painted in a light color; specifically, blue or yellow.

Colon.   Use a colon to introduce a list of items or a general statement.

- We bought the following items at the store: string, paint, glue, and pencils.
- Some of the employees had a second job: three of them, for example, taught classes part-time.

Quotation Marks.   When the quotation mark is used with a comma or a period, the comma or period is always keyed inside the final quotation mark.

- "Progress," the chairman said, "follows planning and hard work."

Short Quote.   Use a comma to introduce a short quote.

- Uncle Charles said, "We will be leaving at noon."
- My sister said, "I hope you have a good trip."

Long Quote.   Use a colon to introduce a long quote.

- The speaker said: "We all need to be more aware of our heritage and what it means to us. Our ancestors worked hard for our freedom. Let us be certain that we maintain that same freedom for our children and our grandchildren."

Question Mark.   The quotation mark precedes the question mark if the quoted matter is not a question.

- Why did Jim say, "I don't want to go along"?
- Didn't he obtain a great deal of fame and fortune as "The Lone Eagle"?
- He asked, "Where are you going?"
- "Will we be able to leave from here?" Jim asked.

Quotation Within a Quotation. To indicate a quotation within a quotation, use the single quotation mark (the apostrophe).

- Marty said, "I want to read the article, 'Telecommuting is In.'"

Special Emphasis. Words or phrases in a sentence may be enclosed in quotation marks when the writer desires to call attention to them.

- We all should eat less "junk food."

Hyphens. A hyphen is used in such expressions as *well-known* and *good-looking* when they are compound modifiers preceding a noun. That is, if a noun follows the expression, hyphens are necessary; if no noun follows, no hyphens are used. No hyphen is used when the first word of the compound modifier ends in *ly*.

- The lecturer was well known.
- He is a well-known lecturer.
- It is a widely read magazine.

Apostrophe. The apostrophe shows ownership or possession.

Singular Nouns Not Ending in S. To form the possessive of a singular noun not ending in *s*, add an apostrophe and *s*.

- The child's book is on the floor.
- Mary's report was very good.

Singular Nouns Ending in S. To form the possessive of a singular noun that ends in *s* or the *s* sound and is of *one syllable only*, add an apostrophe and *s*.

- The boss's telephone is ringing.
- Mr. Burns's report is due tomorrow.
- Miss Race's application came in the mail yesterday.

To form the possessive of a singular noun that ends in *s* or the *s* sound (except *ce* or *se*) and is of *two or more syllables*, add only an apostrophe.

- Mrs. Perkins' address is in the phone book.
- Miss Williams' car is in the garage.
- Horace's testimony was not clear.
- Miss Althouse's car is new.

Plural Nouns Not Ending in S. To form the possessive of a plural noun that does not end in *s*, add *'s*.

- The children's shoes are on sale.
- The men's clothing is quite expensive.

Plural Nouns Ending in S. To form the possessive of a plural noun that ends in *s*, add an apostrophe.

- The ladies' hats blew away because of the wind.

Company and Organization Names. Usually, company and organization names omit the apostrophe.

- The meeting was held at the Farmers National Bank.
- The Teachers College faculty will meet in the Union Building.

Common Possession. When common possession is to be shown for two or more persons, show possession with the last name only.

- Benson and Anderson's book is expensive.

Compound Expressions. The apostrophe is added to the last word of a compound expression.

- His father-in-law's home is on the left side of the street.

Possessive Pronouns. Possessive pronouns such as *ours*, *theirs*, *yours*, *its*, and *hers* do not take an apostrophe. *It's* is a contraction for *it is*.

- The ball is hers.
- The company reported that its productivity is increasing.

Books and Magazines. Underscore the title of a book or magazine.

- Your <u>Reader's Digest</u> subscription has just expired.
- Where is the <u>Handbook for the Medical Secretary</u>?

Title of an Article. The title of an article should be placed within quotation marks.

- "The Art of Buying a New Car" is an excellent article to read.

PURCHASE ORDER FORMAT

A *purchase order* is an external form used to order merchandise from vendors outside of Allied Technology Corporation. It contains the following information: purchase order number; order date; terms; shipping arrangements; and quantity ordered, description, and cost of each of the products. It also includes the total cost of all products ordered. Purchase orders can be produced automatically by the computer since the inventory and accounts payable master files have been created. The computer can also update the inventory and accounts payable master files.

Allied Technology Corporation

2323 North Hamilton Avenue • Omaha, NE 68144-0111
(402) 555-5555 • Fax (402) 555-5444 • E-mail hfm@aolemc.com

Purchase Order

To: Purchase Order No.:
                             Date:
                             Terms:
                             Shipped Via:

Quantity	Description	Price	Per	Total

RECORDS MANAGEMENT

Allied Technology Corporation uses an alphabetic filing system. This system requires a knowledge of alphabetic rules for filing, or indexing. Our company follows standard filing rules based on those recommended by the Association of Record Managers and Administrators, Inc. (ARMA). Following is a list of the rules and some examples of each.

RULE 1: INDEXING ORDER OF UNITS

A. Personal Names

A personal name is indexed in this manner: (1) the surname (last name) is the key unit, (2) the given name (first name) or initial is the second unit, and (3) the middle name or initial is the third unit. If determining the surname is difficult, consider the last name as the surname.

A unit consisting of just an initial precedes a unit that consists of a complete name beginning with the same letter—*nothing before something*. Punctuation is omitted.

Filing Segment / **Indexing Order of Units**

Name	Key Unit	Unit 2	Unit 3
Barbara N. Shelley	SHELLEY	BARBARA	N
Stephen K. Shelly	SHELLY	STEPHEN	K
Dreana Lee Siebert	SIEBERT	DREANA	LEE

B. Business Names

Business names are indexed *as written* using letterheads or trademarks as guides. Each word in a business name is a separate unit. Business names containing personal names are indexed as written.

Filing Segment / **Indexing Order of Units**

Name	Key Unit	Unit 2	Unit 3	Unit 4
Sam Shade Freight Company	SAM	SHADE	FREIGHT	COMPANY
Shade Metal Working	SHADE	METAL	WORKING	
Silly Salley Toy Shop	SILLY	SALLEY	TOY	SHOP

RULE 2: MINOR WORDS AND SYMBOLS IN BUSINESS NAMES

Articles, prepositions, conjunctions, and symbols are considered separate indexing units. Symbols are considered as spelled in full. When the word *the* appears as the first word of a business name, it is considered the last indexing unit.

Filing Segment / **Indexing Order of Units**

Name	Key Unit	Unit 2	Unit 3	Unit 4
A Cutting Place	A	CUTTING	PLACE	
Bonzo the Clown	BONZO	THE	CLOWN	
The $ Smart Shop	DOLLAR	SMART	SHOP	THE

RULE 3: PUNCTUATION AND POSSESSIVES

All punctuation is disregarded when indexing personal and business names. Commas, periods, hyphens, apostrophes, dashes, exclamation points, question marks, quotation marks, and diagonals (/) are disregarded, and names are indexed as written.

Filing Segment	Indexing Order of Units			
Name	*Key Unit*	*Unit 2*	*Unit 3*	*Unit 4*
Alice's Custom Designs	ALICES	CUSTOM	DESIGNS	
"A-OK" Pilot Shop	AOK	PILOT	SHOP	
Whodunit? Mystery Tours	WHODUNIT	MYSTERY	TOURS	

RULE 4: SINGLE LETTERS AND ABBREVIATIONS

A. Personal Names

Initials in personal names are considered separate indexing units. Abbreviations of personal names (Wm., Jos., Thos.) and nicknames (Liz, Bill) are indexed as they are written.

B. Business Names

Single letters in business and organization names are indexed as written. If single letters are separated by spaces, index each letter as a separate unit. An acronym (a word formed from the first or first few letters of several words, such as ARMA or ARCO) is indexed as one unit regardless of punctuation or spacing. Abbreviated words (Mfg., Corp., Inc.) and names (IBM, GE) are indexed as one unit regardless of punctuation or spacing. Radio and television station call letters (WBAP, KRDO) are indexed as one unit.

Filing Segment	Indexing Order of Units			
Name	*Key Unit*	*Unit 2*	*Unit 3*	*Unit 4*
I C I Realty	I	C	I	REALTY
IBM	IBM			
KOGO Television	KOGO	TELEVISION		

RULE 5: TITLES AND SUFFIXES

A. Personal Names

A title before a name (Dr., Miss, Mr., Mrs., Ms., Prof.), a seniority suffix after a name (II, III, Jr., Sr.), or a professional suffix after a name (CRM, DDS, Mayor, D.D., Ph.D., Senator) is the last indexing unit. Numeric suffixes (II, III) are filed before alphabetic suffixes (Jr., Mayor, Senator, Sr.). If a name contains both a title and a suffix, the title is the last unit.

Royal and religious titles followed by either a given name or a surname only (Father Leo, Princess Anne) are indexed and filed as written.

Filing Segment   Indexing Order of Units

Name	Key Unit	Unit 2	Unit 3	Unit 4
Father John	FATHER	JOHN		
Ms. Ada Johnson, CPA	JOHNSON	ADA	CPA	MS
John P. Smith II	SMITH	JOHN	P	II

B. *Business Names*

Titles in business names are indexed as written.

Filing Segment   Indexing Order of Units

Name	Key Unit	Unit 2	Unit 3	Unit 4
Aunt Sally's Cookie Shop	AUNT	SALLYS	COOKIE	SHOP
Dr. Carla's Chimney Works	DR	CARLAS	CHIMNEY	WORKS
Mrs. Mom's Day Care	MRS	MOMS	DAY	CARE

RULE 6: PREFIXES— ARTICLES AND PARTICLES

A foreign name or particle in a personal or business name is combined with the part of the name following it to form a single indexing unit. Thus, the indexing order is not affected by a space between a prefix and the rest of the name.

Filing Segment   Indexing Order of Units

Name	Key Unit	Unit 2	Unit 3	Unit 4
Betty DuBarry's Pro Shop	BETTY	DUBARRYS	PRO	SHOP
Gary Del Carpio	DELCARPIO	GARY		
Joseph Ste. Cyr	STECYR	JOSEPH		

RULE 7: NUMBERS IN BUSINESS NAMES

Numbers spelled out in business names (Seven Acres Inn) are filed alphabetically. Numbers written in digits are filed before alphabetic letters or words (B4 Photographers comes before Beleau Building Co.). Names with numbers written in digits in the first units are filed in ascending order (lowest to highest number) before alphabetic names (229 Shop, 534 Club, Bank of Chicago). Arabic numerals are filed before Roman numerals (2, 3, II, III).

Names with inclusive numbers (33–37) are arranged by the first digit(s) only (33). Names with numbers appearing in other than the first position are filed alphabetically and immediately before a similar name without a number (Pier 36 Cafe, Pier and Port Cafe).

When indexing numerals that contain *st, d,* and *th* (1st, 2d, 3d, 4th), ignore the letter endings and consider only the digits (1, 2, 3, 4).

Filing Segment	Indexing Order of Units			
Name	*Key Unit*	*Unit 2*	*Unit 3*	*Unit 4*
7 Day Food Mart	7	DAY	FOOD	MART
205 Auto Repairs	205	AUTO	REPAIRS	
The 500 De La Rose Shop	500	DELAROSE	SHOP	THE

RULE 8: ORGANIZATIONS AND INSTITUTIONS

Banks and other financial institutions, clubs, colleges, hospitals, hotels, lodges, magazines, motels, museums, newspapers, religious institutions, schools, unions, universities, and other organizations and institutions are indexed and filed according to the names written on their letterheads.

Filing Segment	Indexing Order of Units			
Name	*Key Unit*	*Unit 2*	*Unit 3*	*Unit 4*
1st Christian Church	1	CHRISTIAN	CHURCH	
Assn. of Iron Workers	ASSN	OF	IRON	WORKERS
JFK High School	JFK	HIGH	SCHOOL	

RULE 9: IDENTICAL NAMES

When personal names and names of businesses, institutions, and organizations are identical (including the titles as explained in Rule 5), the filing order is determined by the address. Compare addresses in the following order:

1. City names
2. State or province names (if city names are identical)
3. Street names; include *Avenue, Boulevard, Drive, Street,* etc. (if city and state names are identical)
   a. When the first units of street names are written in digits (18th Street), the names are considered in ascending numeric order (1, 2, 3) and placed together before alphabetic street names (18th Street, 24th Avenue, 36 Grand Blvd., Academy Blvd.).
   b. Street names with compass directions (North, South, East, and West) are considered as written (SE Park Avenue, South Park Avenue). Street numbers written as digits after compass directions are considered before alphabetic street names (East 8th, East Main, Sandusky, SE Eighth, Southeast Eighth).
4. House or building numbers (if city, state, and street names are identical)
   a. House and building numbers written as digits are considered in ascending numeric order (8 Riverside Terrace, 912 Riverside Terrace) and placed together before spelled-out building names (The Riverside Terrace).

b. If a street address and a building name are included in an address, disregard the building name.

c. ZIP Codes are not considered in determining filing order.

Filing Segment / Indexing Order of Units

Name	*Key Unit*	*Unit 2*	*Unit 3*	*Unit 4*	*Unit 5*
First State Bank Elko, Nevada	FIRST	STATE	BANK	ELKO	NEVADA
My-Own Beauty Shop Miami, FL	MYOWN	BEAUTY	SHOP	MIAMI	FL

Name	*Key Unit*	*Unit 2*	*Unit 3*	*Unit 4*	*Unit 5*	*Unit 6*
May's Cafe 4350 12th St. Tulsa, OK	MAYS	CAFE	TULSA	OK	12	ST

RULE 10: GOVERNMENT NAMES

Government names are indexed first by the name of the primary governmental unit—country, state, county, or city. Next, index the distinctive name of the department, bureau, office, or board, including the city, state, etc., if that is part of the name. The words *Office of, Department of, Bureau of,* etc., are separate indexing units when they are part of the official name.

A. Federal

The first three indexing units of a United States (federal) government agency name are *United States Government*.

Key Unit	*Unit 2*	*Unit 3*
UNITED	STATES	GOVERNMENT

Filing Segment / Indexing Order of Units

Name	*Unit 4*	*Unit 5*	*Unit 6*	*Unit 7*	*Unit 8*
Portland Office General Accounting Office	GENERAL	ACCOUNTING	OFFICE	PORTLAND	OFFICE
Bureau of Prisons Justice Department	JUSTICE	DEPARTMENT	PRISONS	BUREAU	OF

B. State and Local

The first indexing units are the names of the state, province, county, parish, city, town, township, or village. Next, index the most distinctive name of the department, board, bureau, office, or government/political division. The words *State of, County of, City of, Department of,* etc., are added only *if needed* for clarity and if in the official name. Each word is considered a separate indexing unit.

Filing Segment	Indexing Order of Units					
Name	*Key Unit*	*Unit 2*	*Unit 3*	*Unit 4*	*Unit 5*	*Unit 6*
Banking Office						
Dept. of Commerce						
(State Government)						
Juneau, AK	ALASKA	COMMERCE	DEPT	OF	BANKING	OFFICE
Highway Div.						
Benton County						
Corvallis, OR	BENTON	COUNTY	HIGHWAY	DIV		

C. Foreign

The distinctive English name is the first indexing unit for foreign government names. Then, index the remainder of the formal name of the government, *if needed* and if it is in the official name (CHINA REPUBLIC OF). Branches, departments, and divisions follow in order by their distinctive names. State colonies, provinces, cities, and other divisions of foreign governments are filed by their distinctive or official names as spelled in English.

Foreign Government Names	English Translation in Indexed Order
Jumhuriyah Misr al-Arabiya	EGYPT ARAB REPUBLIC OF
Republique Francaise	FRENCH REPUBLIC
Bharat	INDIA REPUBLIC OF

RESOURCES

Sources of information

Public library
Company library
College or university libraries
Government publications
Computerized information services

Reference tools

Abstracting services

Almanacs—provide informational summaries on many topics
- *Information Please Almanac*
- *Reader's Digest Almanac*
- *World Almanac*
- *Book of Facts*

Atlases—provide geographical, commercial, and political data, including maps
- *Goode's World Atlas*
- *Rand McNally Commercial Atlas and Marketing Guide*

Biographies (for business)—provide dictionary listings of prominent businesspeople and their corporations
- *Poor's Register of Corporations*
- *Directors and Executives*
- *Who's Who in America*
- *Who's Who in Commerce and Industry* (international coverage)

Book indexes—provide dictionary catalogs of books, listed by author-title-series
- *Books in Print* (includes publisher and price information)
- *Cumulative Book Index* (world)

Congressional Record—all Senators and Representatives—proceedings and debates of Congress

Dictionaries

Directories of companies, organizations, individuals

Dun and Bradstreet credit services

Encyclopedias—provide general background information and comprehensive accumulation of data

Financial reports
- *Moody's Investors Service*
- *Standard and Poor's Services (Financial)*
- *Industry Surveys*
- *Stock Reports*

General periodical indexes
- *Ayer Directory of Publications*
- *Reader's Guide to Periodical Literature*
- *Ulrich's International Periodicals Directory*

Informational services
- *Directory of Business and Financial Services*
- *International Who's Who*

Newspapers and periodicals
- *Barrons—Investor's Magazine* by Dow Jones & Co., Inc. (weekly)
- *Business Week*
- *Forbes* (semi-monthly)
- *The Wall Street Journal*
- *Fortune*—on specific industries and business leaders

- *National Observer*—world affairs, economic and political developments
- *Nation's Business*—by Chamber of Commerce—political and general topics

Secretarial reference materials
- *Secretarial Handbook*
- *Word Finder*

Special indexes
- *Applied Science and Technology Index*
- *Index to Legal Periodicals*
- *New York Times Index*
- *Wall Street Journal Index*

Subscription information services
- *Kiplinger Washington Newsletter*

Telephone directory—area codes and time zones

U.S. Government sources
- *Congressional Report*—speeches, debates, and records of vote
- *Congressional Quarterly*—recording all legislation
- *Congressional Staff Directory*
- *The Monthly Catalog of United States Government Publications*
- *Who's Who in American Politics*

ZIP Code book

SALUTATIONS COMMONLY USED

To one person when name, gender, and courtesy title preference are known:

- Dear Mr. Chambers
- Dear Mrs. Game
- Dear Ms. Champion
- Dear Miss Wellington

To one person when name is known but gender is unknown:

- Dear A. C. Phelps
- Dear Terry Parks

To one person when name is unknown but gender is known:

- Dear Madam
- Dear Sir

To one woman when courtesy title preference is unknown:

- Dear Ms. Martin
- Dear Rachelle Martin

To two or more men:

- Dear Mr. Andrews and Mr. Jenner
- Gentlemen

To two or more women:

- Dear Mrs. Benjamin, Ms. Smith, and Miss Brown
- Dear Misses Gray and Art
- Dear Mrs. James and Mrs. Schultz
- Dear Miss Gray and Miss Art
- Dear Ms. Gerkin and Ms. Abbot

To a woman and a man:

- Dear Ms. Backer and Mr. White
- Dear Mrs. Kirk and Mr. Arp
- Dear Mr. Frank and Miss Leopold
- Dear Mr. and Mrs. Grant

To several people:

- Dear Mr. Akers, Mrs. Brent, Ms. Clark, Mr. Delta, and Miss Rosen
- Dear Friends (or Members, Colleagues, Consultants, Stockholders, etc.)

To an organization composed entirely of men:

- Gentlemen

To an organization composed entirely of women:

- Ladies

To an organization composed of men and women:

- Ladies and Gentlemen
- Gentlemen and Ladies

SECOND-PAGE HEADINGS AND PUNCTUATION STYLES OF LETTERS

Be sure to carry over at least two lines from the first page of the letter plus the closing lines. Never carry over a divided word. Leave two blank lines below the heading and continue keying the letter. Use plain paper of the same quality as the letterhead. Use the same left and right margins that you used on the first page.

When beginning the second page of a letter, leave a 1-inch top margin before keying the recipient's name, page number, and date.

You may use either of the following two styles:

| Atlantic Supply Company | 2 | Current Date |

Atlantic Supply Company
Page 2
Current Date

Two main punctuation styles are used at ATC.

MIXED PUNCTUATION

Using this format, a colon follows the salutation and a comma appears after the complimentary close. No other punctuation marks are used except those concluding an abbreviation or those appearing within the body of the letter. For example:

Dear Mr. Smith:

Sincerely,

OPEN PUNCTUATION

Using this format, no closing punctuation marks follow the salutation or the complimentary close. Punctuation marks are used only when they conclude an abbreviation or appear within the body of the letter. For example:

Dear Mr. Smith

Sincerely

STATE AND PROVINCIAL ABBREVIATIONS

State	Two-Letter Abbreviation	State	Two-Letter Abbreviation
Alabama	AL	Montana	MT
Alaska	AK	Nebraska	NE
Arizona	AZ	Nevada	NV
Arkansas	AR	New Hampshire	NH
California	CA	New Jersey	NJ
Colorado	CO	New Mexico	NM
Connecticut	CT	New York	NY
Delaware	DE	North Carolina	NC
Florida	FL	North Dakota	ND
Georgia	GA	Ohio	OH
Hawaii	HI	Oklahoma	OK
Idaho	ID	Oregon	OR
Illinois	IL	Pennsylvania	PA
Indiana	IN	Rhode Island	RI
Iowa	IA	South Carolina	SC
Kansas	KS	South Dakota	SD
Kentucky	KY	Tennessee	TN
Louisiana	LA	Texas	TX
Maine	ME	Utah	UT
Maryland	MD	Vermont	VT
Massachusetts	MA	Virginia	VA
Michigan	MI	Washington	WA
Minnesota	MN	West Virginia	WV
Mississippi	MS	Wisconsin	WI
Missouri	MO	Wyoming	WY

Canadian Province Abbreviations

Province	Two-Letter Abbreviation	Province	Two-Letter Abbreviation
Alberta	AB *Regina*	Nova Scotia	NS *Halifax*
British Columbia	BC *Victoria*	Ontario	ON *Toronto*
Labrador	LB *St. John's*	Prince Edward Island	PE *Charlottetown*
Manitoba	MB *Winnipeg*	Quebec	PQ *Quebec City*
New Brunswick	NB *Fredericton*	Saskatchewan	SK *Regina*
Newfoundland	NF *St. John's*	Yukon Territory	YT *Whitehorse*
Northwest Territories	NT *Yellowknife*		

TELEPHONE ETIQUETTE, TIME-WASTERS, TIME MANAGEMENT

Making Calls

- Speak distinctly and slowly.
- Plan the conversation—make notes.
- Place your own calls.
- Give the person being called sufficient time to answer.
- Give sufficient information so the person calling back will know what you want and can assemble the necessary information before your call is returned.
- Check the time difference before calling across the nation or calling internationally.
- Be aware of the best time to place long-distance calls to save money.

Receiving Calls

- Answer the phone as quickly as possible.
- Use a pleasant, helpful voice.
- Identify yourself and your department.
- "May I tell _____ who is calling, please?"
- Ask if the caller wishes to leave a message.
- Write down any message that is left.
- Be sure the name and number are correct.
- Deliver messages promptly.
- Use the "hold" button when leaving the phone for a short time.
- Check back with the caller often if the caller is left waiting.
- Be sure the caller wishes to be transferred.
- Let the caller conclude the conversation.
- If you are going out of the office, let others know when you will be back so such information can be given to callers.
- Take calls for others as efficiently and as courteously as you would expect them to take your calls.

Time-Wasters

- Excessive telephone calls
- Drop-in visitors
- Socializing
- Getting incomplete information
- Failure to delegate
- Lack of a daily plan
- Procrastination
- Giving out information
- Shifting priorities
- Errands

Time Management

- Plan
- Set deadlines
- Think
- Prioritize
- Follow through

TIME ZONE DIFFERENCES

The following chart lists time zone differences between the United States and a number of other countries. To determine the time in the locale being called, add the number of hours listed under your time zone to your current time (or subtract if the number is preceded by a minus sign). (EST = Eastern Standard Time; CST = Central Standard Time; MST = Mountain Standard Time; PST = Pacific Standard Time.) *Note:* Omaha is in the Central time zone.

| | U.S. Time Zones | | | |
Time Difference From U.S to	EST	CST	MST	PST
Belgium	+6	+7	+8	+9
France	+6	+7	+8	+9
Germany	+6	+7	+8	+9
Greece	+7	+8	+9	+10
Guatemala	-1	0	+1	+2
Hong Kong	+13	+14	+15	+16
Ireland	+5	+6	+7	+8
Italy	+6	+7	+8	+9
Japan	+14	+15	+16	+17
Mexico	-1	0	+1	+2
Philippines	+13	+14	+15	+16
Poland	+6	+7	+8	+9
Spain	+6	+7	+8	+9
Sweden	+6	+7	+8	+9
United Kingdom	+5	+6	+7	+8

TRAVEL AND CONFERENCE INFORMATION

All of the executives at Allied Technology Corporation prefer to fly; the company travel agency is called Best Travel Agency. The phone number is 402-555-6776 and the fax number is 402-555-8334. The corporate contact at the agency is Sam Aldrich. Most of the travel arrangements are made by fax, which is more accurate than using verbal communication when referring to flight numbers, departure times, etc.

Best Travel Agency has our special corporate credit card number as well as a list of all the travel details that each executive has requested, such as seat arrangements, special food and drinks, etc. Best Travel Agency also routinely arranges for ground transportation with the Best Service Car Rental Agency whenever one of the executives needs that service. The travel agency knows the make and model of car that each executive prefers and will try to make that kind of car available at the airport when the executive arrives at his/her destination.

The administrative assistant for each executive is responsible for faxing the necessary information (time and place of meeting and desired length of stay) to Best Travel Agency as soon as the executive's travel plans are known. The administrative assistant is also responsible for verifying that the travel agency's arrangements are appropriate for the executive's trip.

The administrative assistant makes all meeting arrangements with the hotel, including reserving hotel rooms for the executive and others attending the meeting; arranging for a conference room; and checking on the availability of all necessary items for the meeting such as phones, overhead projectors, flipcharts and pens, water, and refreshment service. Luncheon and dinner reservations for the conference group also need to be made. After confirming all of the arrangements, the AA must contact all other individuals who will be attending the meeting to let them know of the plans.

When arranging a meeting, be sure to take into consideration the time zone changes, which can affect the travel time as well as the meeting times.

WORD USAGE

Accept, except. *Accept* means to take or receive. *Except* refers to an exclusion of something.

- We cannot *accept* the check since it has been altered.
- No one *except* you knows the password.

Advice, advise. *Advice* is a noun and means a suggestion, an opinion, or a recommendation. *Advise* means to counsel.

- It is often difficult to follow the *advice* of our parents.
- She will *advise* him to take the early bus out of town.

Affect, effect. *Affect* is a verb that means to influence. *Effect* is a noun and means a result or consequence.

- If she receives a pay cut, it will *affect* her spending habits.
- A pay cut will have a negative *effect* on her vacation plans.

All ready, already. *All ready* means to be prepared. *Already* means by this time or before this time.

- We are *all ready* to go to the party.
- We have *already* spent more money than we had planned.

All right, alright. *All right* refers to approval. *Alright* is an informal spelling of *all right* and is not correct.

- It is *all right* for you to go to the movie if you are home by 10 p.m.

Almost, most. *Almost* is an adverb meaning nearly. *Most* is an adjective or adverb meaning the greatest in number or quality.

- Jenna *almost* got an A+ on her test.
- The *most* exciting thing I did all summer was to go to Colorado.

Beside, besides. *Beside* means to be next to or at the side of something. *Besides* means in addition or extra.

- The doctor's office is *beside* the church.
- The mail carrier brought us two packages *besides* the regular mail.

Between, among. *Between* refers to two people or things. *Among* refers to more than two people or things.

- The matter will be settled *between* John and Mary.
- The matter will be settled *among* the four individuals involved.

Can, may. *Can* is the ability to do something. *May* is to give or receive permission to do something.

- I *can* sing three verses of that song without hearing the music.
- I *may* go to the movie if I return by 10 p.m.

Choose, chose. *Choose* is to select or make a choice. *Chose* is past tense for "choose."

- Sally will *choose* the best article for the publication.
- She *chose* the article about the bicycle race.

Disburse, disperse. *Disburse* means to pay out or distribute. *Disperse* means to cause to become widely spread.

- We will *disburse* the money received from the garage sale equally among all of you.
- We will *disperse* this information by e-mail.

Every one, everyone. *Every one* refers to each person in the group. *Everyone* refers to all the people in the group.

- *Every one* in the accident was injured in some way.
- *Everyone* will have to pay the same price.

Forth, fourth. *Forth* means to go forward. *Fourth* is a numeric term.

- The men went *forth* to fight the battle.
- This is the *fourth* time I have given you the prize.

Good, well. *Good* is an adjective meaning skillful, admirable, or having the right qualities. It describes a noun and answers the question "what kind of." *Well* is an adverb telling how something is done. It usually modifies a verb and answers the question "how."

- The dinner was *good*.
- Jim plays golf *well*.

In, into. *In* is a preposition and means within a place. *Into* means to go or put inside of something.

- Lydia is *in* the bedroom.
- They kicked the ball *into* the garage.

Interstate, intrastate. *Interstate* means between states. *Intrastate* means within a state.

- We will be traveling on *Interstate* 80 for most of the trip to California.
- The Nebraska company ships *intrastate* products only.

It's, its. *It's* is the contraction for *it is*. The apostrophe takes the place of the letter "i." The contraction *it's* acts as the subject and the verb of a clause or sentence. *Its* is a possessive pronoun.

- *It's* a good idea.
- The mall and *its* stores attract the people.

Later, latter. *Later* refers to a future time. *Latter* refers to the last thing mentioned.

- We will go to the store *later* than we had planned.
- The *latter* idea seems to be the best one.

Passed, past. *Passed* is a verb meaning to go by. *Past* is a noun or adjective and refers to something that has gone by.

- They *passed* the accident without stopping.
- It is best to put our *past* failures behind us and concentrate on the present.

Precede, proceed. *Precede* means to go before. *Proceed* means to go forward or continue.

- That information should *precede* the summary of the article.
- We will *proceed* with the meeting even though we do not have a quorum.

Quiet, quite. *Quiet* refers to that which is free from noise. *Quite* is an adverb meaning completely or actually.

- A library is usually a good place to study since it is so *quiet*.
- The girls are *quite* willing to make their presentations before the group.

Role, roll. *Role* refers to a part or character. *Roll* is a list of names or something wound around a core.

- She usually plays the *role* of the villain in that play.
- When she called the *roll,* his name was not mentioned.
- The *roll* of string is in the car.

Than, then. *Than* is a conjunction and is used to show comparison. *Then* is an adverb and means at that time.

- Billy is smarter in math *than* Benny.
- We will go to the zoo and *then* to the park.

There, their, they're. *There* is an adverb. It is never used to show ownership. *Their* is used to show ownership. *They're* is the contraction for *they are.*

- *There* is not always a good reason for being late to class.
- *Their* assignment was very short.
- *They're* happy with the grades they received.

To, too, two. *To* is a preposition. *Too* is an adverb meaning also or in excess. *Two* is a numeric term.

- We were willing to go *to* the picnic.
- We were not *too* anxious to go.
- There were *two* of us at the park that day.

Who's, whose. *Who's* is the contraction for *who is. Whose* shows ownership or possession. It is used as a possessive adjective and modifies a noun.

- *Who's* your favorite singer?
- *Whose* bicycle is on the sidewalk?

Monday Assignment
(January 23)

Friday

From the Desk of
Mary Andrews
Human Resources and Development

A
T
C

*Find Customer List No. 56 in the <u>Employees'</u>
<u>Information Manual</u> and find the ZIP Codes
for each city listed. Enter all the information
into a database—use all caps. Sort by ZIP
Code, by company name, and by state. (Use the
company library or call the post office for this
information.) You should have three lists to
give me.*

NEED ON FRIDAY

Mary

(Students: You will need to use a *general ZIP Code*—such as 68501, 80201, 36101—for large
cities since the company names and addresses in Customer List No. 56 are fictional.)

monday

From the Desk of
Mary Andrews
Human Resources and Development

A
T
C

Regarding references for Mrs. Sally Aldrich —

Find the "Request for reference" (reqrefer.ltr) letter on disk and use it as a sample to prepare letters to send to the following three people:

1. Robert Smith, Consultant, Adams Certificates, 1934 State Street, Gretna, NE 68028

2. Betty Belle, President, Best Fashion Designs, 3564 South 114 Street, Omaha, NE 68114

3. Carlos Mendoza, Manager, Burns State Bank, Burns, IA 51503

Be sure to prepare mailing envelopes and enclose return envelopes. I need these by 4:00 today

Mary

Check on envelope

(Students: Use the ATC address in the return block of all envelopes being sent out of the company.)

Wednesday ✓

Mary Andrews

Allied
Technology
Corporation

Human Resources and Development
Department Manager
402-555-4445

Chris--Key an agenda for the seminar entitled ENJOYING
YOUR JOB. Send the agenda to the Printing Department
after I have approved it. Send a copy of the agenda to
each speaker along with a letter of explanation (from
disk--spkconf.ltr) by Wednesday. There are 30
employees who will attend. Speaker information is
listed below:

"Looking On the Bright Side"
Henry Morgen, Manager, Kellie Mfg Firm.
2345 Chicago Avenue   *Put firm name here*   *Write Out*
Omaha, NE 68157

stet "You Can Get There From Here"
Beth Brown, Vice President, Health, Inc.
2533 "Q" Street   *Next Line*
Millard, NE 68137

"Improving Your Communication Skills"
Martha Jenks, Communications Chair,
University of Nebraska, 60 and Dodge, Omaha, NE 68103

"Your Health Plays a Part, Too"
Beth Brown

"Working It Out Together"
Martha Jenks

Mary Andrews

Allied Technology Corporation

**Human Resources and Development
Department Manager
402-555-4445**

Allied Technology Corporation

In-Service Program

Chris -
See how attractive you
can make the agenda.
MA

Agenda Information:
Conference Room No. 38
8:30 a.m. - 4:30 p.m. 5:00
Monday, July 10, ---- In-Service Program

"Getting Along Enjoying Your Job   caps — fancy

Put speaker name and title, company name, city, state

8:30 - 9:00	Coffee Service
9:00 - 9:15	Greetings from me
9:15 - 10:15	"Looking on the bright side" by _____
10:15 - 10:30	Break
10:30 - 11:45	"You can get there from here" by _____
11:45 - 1:00	Lunch Break
1:00 - 2:00	"Improving Your Communications Skills" by ____
2:00 - 3:00	"Your health plays a part, too" by _____
3:00 - 3:15	Break
3:15 - 4:30	"Working it out together" by _____
4:30 - 5:00	Group Discussion and Questions

Just the speaker names here

Line up times

Wednesday

From the Desk of
Mary Andrews
Human Resources and Development

A
T
C

We will be offering a series of courses for our personnel during the next several months. We need an attractive flyer to be sent to all departments. Be sure to show me your first draft—then we will talk about any changes before you finalize it.

Be sure to place courses in categories such as Communications, Professional Development, Travel, etc. Add a phone number for registration purposes. Mary Pare will be in charge of that. Her extension is 3347.

—I need the first draft by Friday!

...UASION

4 Sessions beginning May 25
Thursdays, 1:00-5:00 p.m.

...nipulative approach allows persua-
...from the basis of a common under-
...l goals. Arguments, evidence, roles,
...d nonverbal persuasion are empha-
...rsuasion is designed for individuals
...ent, or supervision.

...COMMUNICATIONS FOR OFFICE

...sions beginning June 6
...ays and Thursdays,
...a.m.-5:00 p.m.

...sions beginning June 7
...esdays and Fridays,
...a.m.-5:00 p.m.

...to use a singular verb and when to
...you hesitant about where to place
...or semicolons? Have basic filing
...call? Join the group for a compre-
...tion, spelling, grammar, and usage;
..., plurals, and possessives; business
...s; proofreading, editing, and word
...ion and word divisions, and misused

...UDIO SLIDE PRESENTATIONS

3 Sessions beginning June 15
Thursdays, 1:00-5:00 p.m.

...pert a step-by-step method to produce
...natic sound-accompanied slide shows.
...provide a theoretical base for analyz-
...and selecting equipment. It will in-
...lopment, slide progressing, and sound
...asic knowledge of photography and
...erience are strongly recommended for
...EA4-0134

...or conflict will learn the causes of conflict and the
most common barriers to its resolution. Communication skills for clarifying conflict, identifying nonverbals
that signal conflict, and the use of questions to get it
out in the open will be practiced. Disagreeing, confronting, fogging, and broken-record techniques will
be evaluated as team members learn to "fight fair."

HANDS-ON COMPUTERS: THE PERSONAL TOUCH

(DA4-0089) 10 Sessions beginning May 24
Wednesdays, 8:00 a.m.-5:00 p.m.

(DA4-0090) 10 Sessions beginning October 7
Saturdays, 8:00 a.m.-5:00 p.m.

This ten-session course for beginners will give you an
understanding of computer components and terminology
while providing hands-on experience in three common word
processing programs. Computer hardware and functions
will be described as well as criteria for evaluating and
comparing different microcomputer systems. No prior
computer experience necessary. Enrollment limited.

BASIC SINGLE-CAMERA VIDEO PRODUCTION

(EA4-0049) 1 Session, June 16
Friday, 1:00-5:00 p.m.

This half-day seminar emphasizes a hands-on experience in small-format video production techniques. It
is designed for those who have had no experience or
only limited experience with video production. Part
of the session will be devoted to the development of
creative elements from concept to finished product.
Actual recording techniques will be covered. Teams
of three to five participants will actually produce a
short video program. All materials are provided.
Enrollment limited to 16.

Started

POSITIONING YOURSELF: A CAREER PLANNING WORKSHOP

(EA4-0079)   4 Sessions beginning May 3
Wednesdays, 1:00-5:00 p.m.

This course is about how to build a career without waiting for an organization to do it for you. Designed to demonstrate that career planning is a systematic and learnable process, this course will help you discover professional strengths and undeveloped skills, identify the job market and appropriate job titles to meet your career goals, and "market" your skills through interviewing and resume writing.

TIME MANAGEMENT

(EA4-0037)   2 Sessions beginning May 9
Tuesdays, 9:00 a.m.-12:00 noon

Do you make priority decisions in your life? Understand the principles of time management in order to gain control of your time. You will learn skills to put you in charge of time both in your professional and personal life.

PETITE WOMEN: STRETCH TO NEW HEIGHTS THROUGH DRESS

(AA4-0075)   1 Session, May 6
Saturday, 2:00-5:00 p.m.

Are you 5'4" or under and looking for ideas for dressing taller? In this workshop we will discuss ways to counter the "cute" image and determine your most flattering look. Learn about specific needs of the short figure; develop a personal dress style; and get tips on where to shop and what to look for, from suits to shoes.

CONSTRUCTIVE CONFLICT RESOLUTION FOR MANAGERS

(EA4-0082)   4 Sessions beginning May 18
Thursdays, 8:00 a.m.-5:00 p.m.

Middle managers seeking skills in the constructive use of conflict will learn the causes of conflict and the most common barriers to its resolution. Communication skills for clarifying conflict, identifying nonverbals that signal conflict, and the use of questions to get it out in the open will be practiced. Disagreeing, confronting, fogging, and broken-record techniques will be evaluated as team members learn to "fight fair."

HANDS-ON COMPUTERS: THE PERSONAL TOUCH

(DA4-0089)   10 Sessions beginning May 24
Wednesdays, 8:00 a.m.-5:00 p.m.

(DA4-0090)   10 Sessions beginning October 7
Saturdays, 8:00 a.m.-5:00 p.m.

This ten-session course for beginners will give you an understanding of computer components and terminology while providing hands-on experience in three common word processing programs. Computer hardware and functions will be described as well as criteria for evaluating and comparing different microcomputer systems. No prior computer experience necessary. Enrollment limited.

POSITIVE PERSUASION

(EA4-0039)   4 Sessions beginning May 25
Thursdays, 1:00-5:00 p.m.

Use of the nonmanipulative approach allows persuasion to take place from the basis of a common understanding of defined goals. Arguments, evidence, roles, self-persuasion, and nonverbal persuasion are emphasized. Positive Persuasion is designed for individuals in sales, management, or supervision.

EFFECTIVE BUSINESS COMMUNICATIONS FOR OFFICE PERSONNEL

(DA4-0080)   8 Sessions beginning June 6
Tuesdays and Thursdays,
8:00 a.m.-5:00 p.m.

(DA4-0081)   8 Sessions beginning June 7
Wednesdays and Fridays,
8:00 a.m.-5:00 p.m.

Have you forgotten when to use a singular verb and when to use a plural verb? Are you hesitant about where to place commas, quotation marks, or semicolons? Have basic filing rules slipped away from recall? Join the group for a comprehensive review of punctuation, spelling, grammar, and usage; abbreviations, contractions, plurals, and possessives; business letters, memos, and reports; proofreading, editing, and word processing skills; hyphenation and word divisions, and misused and confused words.

PRODUCING AUDIO SLIDE PRESENTATIONS

(EA4-0135)   3 Sessions beginning June 15
Thursdays, 1:00-5:00 p.m.

Learn from an expert a step-by-step method to produce manual and automatic sound-accompanied slide shows. The course will provide a theoretical base for analyzing an audience and selecting equipment. It will include script development, slide progressing, and sound coordination. Basic knowledge of photography and scriptwriting experience are strongly recommended for this class. See EA4-0134

BASIC SINGLE-CAMERA VIDEO PRODUCTION

(EA4-0049)   1 Session, June 16
Friday, 1:00-5:00 p.m.

This half-day seminar emphasizes a hands-on experience in small-format video production techniques. It is designed for those who have had no experience or only limited experience with video production. Part of the session will be devoted to the development of creative elements from concept to finished product. Actual recording techniques will be covered. Teams of three to five participants will actually produce a short video program. All materials are provided. Enrollment limited to 16.

SURVIVAL SPANISH FOR TRAVELERS

(EA4-0070)   5 Sessions beginning April 22
Saturdays, 9:00 a.m.-12:00 noon

For travelers to Spanish-speaking countries who do not plan to travel with a tour guide, this course will provide basic Spanish for commonly experienced situations. Vocabulary and pronunciation practice for surviving in customs offices, hotels, restaurants, banks, theaters, airports, and train stations will be included. Cultural "do's and don'ts" will also be discussed.

THE ART OF DELEGATING

(EA4-0033)   2 Sessions beginning March 14
Tuesdays, 9:00 a.m.-12:00 noon

Many managers hesitate to delegate either because they see no need to do it ("I can do it more quickly myself"), they don't know exactly how to delegate ("how can I hand this off?"), or they simply enjoy doing the task and are reluctant to let anyone else handle it. This is especially true for new supervisors who are now expected to **manage** those tasks that they used to **perform**. This workshop will address the benefits of delegation, typical barriers to effective delegation, and the different degrees of delegation.

CONTROLLING PUBLIC SPEAKING ANXIETY

(EA4-0056)   4 Sessions beginning April 27
Thursdays, 12:00 noon-4:00 p.m.

This course is designed with the understanding that many working people are anxious about public speaking. As a result, they avoid opportunities to present their ideas and their solutions to organizational problems, and thus remain unrecognized for their special talents and hard work. By providing a supportive environment, this course will reduce the fear of making presentations to large and small groups. No previous experience with public speaking is required.

INTRODUCTION TO COMPUTERS

(DA4-0067)   10 Sessions beginning June 24
Saturdays, 9:00-12:00 noon

(DA4-0068)   10 Sessions beginning June 24
Saturdays, 2:00-5:00 p.m.

This is an introductory course in computer technology for people who need (or want) to know about computers. Through lecture and demonstration, you will learn what computers are and how they work; terminology; how computer systems are developed (payroll, inventory, etc.); how to estimate and stay within costs; collection and storage of information; applications in education, business, and industry; and future uses. Includes a section on home computers and a tour of a computing facility. This course is also a useful foundation for those who are considering entering the computing field. Enrollment limited.

EFFECTIVE SURVIVAL SKILLS FOR MANAGERS AND SUPERVISORS

(EA4-0038)   5 Sessions beginning March 23
Thursdays, 8:00 a.m.-5:00 p.m.

This course is designed for managers and supervisors who wish to better understand and perhaps to change their management style for increased effectiveness. It will focus on using new styles to better manage subordinates, bosses, and peers, as well as on using the 80/20 rule for career advancement and personal survival.

SCRIPTWRITING FOR VIDEO OR SLIDE PRESENTATIONS

(EA4-0134)   2 Sessions beginning June 28
Wednesdays, 9:00 a.m.-12:00 noon

This course is designed for people interested in learning the basics of writing scripts for video, film, and slide presentations. There will be instruction and beginning exercises in writing for the ear, conceptualization, and script style and form. Strongly recommended as a prerequisite to "Producing Audio Slide Presentations."

MEDIA KNOW-HOW: PROMOTING YOUR NONPROFIT ORGANIZATION

(EA4-0040)   8 Sessions beginning August 1
Tuesdays and Thursdays,
10:00 a.m.-4:00 p.m.

Have you ever wondered why some nonprofit organizations always seem to get their names in the newspapers, their public service announcements broadcast, and their fund-raising events publicized? The answer is preplanning, know-how, and follow-through.

This course is designed to help media representatives from nonprofit organizations in these three areas. The first two-thirds of the course will provide advice from professionals in the fields of news, advertising, photography, and commercial music. The last portion of the course will allow you to discuss the specific problems of your organization with the moderator and classmates.

INTELLIGENT INVESTMENTS

(EA4-0036)   8 Sessions beginning July 11
Tuesdays, 3:00-5:00 p.m.

Become knowledgeable about investing in the stock market. This course explores investment analysis for the beginner and for those with limited experience. Primary emphasis is placed on common stocks and on the development of individual investment goals and objectives. Includes a field trip to a brokerage house.

SURVIVAL FRENCH FOR TRAVELERS

(EA4-0069)   5 Sessions beginning July 5
Wednesdays, 5:30-7:30 p.m.

For travelers to France, who do not plan to go everywhere with a tour guide, this course will provide basic French for commonly experienced situations. Vocabulary and pronunciation practice for surviving in customs offices, hotels, restaurants, banks, theaters, airports, and train stations will be included. Cultural "do's and don'ts" will also be discussed.

Monday Powerpoint

Mary Andrews

*Allied
Technology
Corporation*

**Human Resources and Development
Department Manager
402-555-4445**

RUSH—NEED BY 3 P.M. TODAY (MONDAY)

I need 2 transparency masters of the following items for a talk I am giving today. Title = "Qualifications of a Professional Administrative Assistant from a Manager's Viewpoint."

Use a bullet for each item. Divide the items so that half will be on one transparency and half on the other. Be sure that the print is large enough to read at a distance because this will be presented in the large conference room.

A Professional Administrative Assistant:

enjoys his/her job

possesses tact and diplomacy

is always dressed professionally

has a positive attitude

is cooperative

stays cool under pressure

anticipates the needs of the employer

uses good judgment

has good telephone manners

is able to prioritize

communicates well orally and in writing

is accurate and conscientious

Monday

Mary Andrews

*Allied
Technology
Corporation*

**Human Resources and Development
Department Manager
402-555-4445**

Chris— Please prepare a memo for all Department Supervisors telling them about four workshops that will meet from 9 until Noon on March 13, 20, 27, and April 3 in Conference Room 10A.

The workshops will allow supervisors to interact and to share concepts and ideas with the others in attendance. The workshops will explore such areas as leadership, improving and maintaining employee performance, utilizing effective follow-up actions, and utilizing effective corrective action. Participants are expected to attend all four sessions and can call Mary Pare at X3347 to register.

Send the memo today (Monday).

Mary

wednesday

From the Desk of
Mary Andrews
Human Resources and Development

A
T
C

Revise the State Abbreviation page from the Company Procedures Manual. Add the capital city for each state (by Wednesday). The information should be in the company's Office Handbook or check our company's reference library or your computer for the information.

Mary

(Students: Ask your instructor for an office reference book or an atlas to research this information. You may also find the information on your computer.)

Friday

Mary Andrews

Allied Technology Corporation

Human Resources and Development
Department Manager
402-555-4445

Monday—Check the <u>Employees' Information Manual</u> and gather the following information so that we can determine how much vacation time everyone in our department is entitled to. Key the information into a database using the following fields: Social Security No., Name, Starting Date, Today's Date, Vacation Days Available, and Department. Sort by Employee Name.

Note—Employees get one week for the first six months of the year that they work and another week for the second six months they work, for a total of two weeks maximum per year. After they have worked here for five years, they receive three weeks' vacation time.

Prepare memos letting each employee know how much vacation time he/ she has for this year and asking each employee to let you know his/her preferred vacation time. Place each memo in an envelope with the name of the individual on the envelope and put it in the company mail. (See directions for addressing envelopes for company mail in the <u>Company Procedures Manual.</u>) When you receive the necessary information, prepare a chart showing when each employee wants to take his/her vacation. I need that information on Friday.

Also—fill in as many blanks as you can on the Vacation Request Form for each employee in our department. I would also like to have these on Friday.

Mary

(Students: Do as much as you can with the information provided here. You will receive more information later in the simulation.)

ATC

INTEROFFICE MEMORANDUM

SKiP

To: Mary Andrews
From: Cindy Spring
Date: January 23, ——
Subject: Plan Your Business Functions Carefully

Please send me an outline of the article titled "Plan Your Business Functions Carefully," which we discussed at a recent meeting.

dg

Chris- This article is on disk (busfunct.art). Prepare an outline of it and send it to Cindy sometime this week. Refer to the sample outline format in the Company Procedures Manual.

M A

Mary Andrews

Allied
Technology
Corporation

Human Resources and Development
Department Manager
402-555-4445

Key the following message and send a copy to each of the other four department managers. The list of dept. mgrs. is in the <u>Employees' Information Manual</u>. Key "Suggestions Anyone?" in the Subject area. Put it in the company mail today.

The Human Resources and Development Department wants to hear from you about ways that we can be more helpful. Your comments, criticisms, or suggestions will be welcomed as we attempt to please the employees at Allied Technology Corporation. We know that there are ways we can improve our services; you are probably aware of additional ways we can be of help to you or your department. You may call x4445, e-mail at mandrews@atc.ind, or send an anonymous message through company mail to Mary Andrews, Human Resources and Development Department, Manager.

monday

From the Desk of
Mary Andrews
Human Resources and Development

A
T
C

I need ~~three~~ one No. 10 envelopes addressed to *each* of the branch managers and *one* for the CEO. Check the _Employees' Information Manual_ for the addresses and the _Company Procedures Manual_ for directions on addressing envelopes.

Please do it today.

From the Desk of
Mary Andrews
Human Resources and Development

A T C

I have dictated an article entitled "Ethics." Transcribe it on plain paper and send a copy to each department manager. Prepare an Interoffice Memorandum to go with the article. It should say the following:

Attached is an article entitled "Ethics." The Human Resources and Development Department is available to set up a training program for your employees on this topic. We need three weeks' advance notice to set up a two-hour training session. Call Mary Pare at x3347 to make the arrangements.

Please do it today.

12M-M

From the Desk of
Mary Andrews
Human Resources and Development

A
T
C

Chris—

An article entitled "Passing On the Family Business Successfully" is on the cassette tape that I put in your office. It should be good information for some of our customers. Transcribe the tape and send a copy to each of the branch managers. Include a memo from me with a brief message indicating that I think the article will have merit for some of our customers. Be sure to get it in the mail today.

Mary

Tuesday Assignment (January 24)

From the Desk of
Mary Andrews
Human Resources and Development

A
T
C

Pg 85

Key the article regarding transition from vacation to work and send a copy to each department manager. Attach a memo to each one telling him/her to give copies to his/her employees. Try to finish this today (Tuesday) so it can get in the company mail tomorrow.

Mary

mail
merge
To: line

Mary Andrews

Allied
Technology
Corporation

Human Resources and Development
Department Manager
402-555-4445

indent all ¶ s *lc* *lc* *Bold heading, Larger print*

Planning Eases Transition From Vacation To Work

Experts say that there is usually a two-day lag in production time when an employee returns to work. Part of the problem is lack of sleep and part is getting up to speed on what's going on at work.

There seems to be a correlation between the length of a vacation and how hard it is to get back into the daily grind. The longer the time off, the tougher it is to make the transition. # It is advisable not to call clients or make any big decisions for a couple of days after returning to the office.

Most of us look forward to vacations and, assumming we have a good time, we are resistant to the idea of going back to work--especially when we realize that it will be another year before we get another vacation.

Insert ¶ B

To avoid the burnout problemk consider dividing your vacation time into mini-holidays so you can look forward to another vacation sooner than a year away.

Insert ¶ A *home base*

¶ B Get back to work at least a day early to give yourself a chance to unpack, organise, recover from jet lag, and relax.
z

¶ A Before you leave on vacation, make an agenda for what you need to do when you return. That way your first day back will have more direction to it. ¶Your employer will be happy to work with you to arrange the best schedule and most enjoyable vacation time. In order to achieve a good vacation schedule, talk it over with your employer early in the year so that apropriate arrangements can be made.
sp

Have a great vacation!!
bold

Wednesday

From the Desk of
Mary Andrews
Human Resources and Development

A T C

Chris—Here is the seminar program we used in Sioux City, Iowa, on March 29 last year. We will be following the same format for the departmental administrative assistants on June 29 this year. Prepare an attractive one-page brochure for my approval.

I need this by 3:00 on Wed.

tri-fold brochure

---

une 29
onference Room G

ke a Difference
(with answers)
(with answers)

sentation

ng

~~2:30 – 2:45   Coffee Break~~

~~2:45 – 3:30~~
2:00-3:00 ──────┌─ Time Management
                              Dress For Success   *lc*
                              Self-Image
                              On-The-Job Cases
                              Minutes
                              Stress
Bold↘   Are You Resisting Progress?
3:00-3:15 Break └─ Human Relations in the Office
                   3:15-4:15 Computers in Business
~~3:00 – 3:45~~   Wrap Up
4:15-4:30
~~3:30   4:00~~   Evaluations and Questions
4:30-5:00

Title larger print and bold < *Our company name at top*

~~Sioux City, Iowa~~
~~Seminar- March 29,~~ ___   *June 29*
Conference Room G

9:00 - 10:00	Punctuation Rules
	Capitalization/Numbers
	~~Transparency--Does Punctuation Make a Difference?~~
	Practice Exercises on Punctuation ~~(with answers)~~
	Practice Exercises on Capitalization ~~(with answers)~~
	Handout--Punctuation Rules
10:00 - 10:30	Office of the Future
10:30 - 10:45	Coffee Break *Bold*
10:45 - 12:00	Records Management
	lc Startling Facts About Paperwork
	Purging Your Files
	Records Management slide/tape presentation
	Records Management Quiz
	Filing Rules and Exercises
12:00 - 1:00	Lunch *Bold*
1:00 - 2:00	Proofreading
	Aids to Successful Proofreading
	Proofreading Exercises
	New Style Formats
	Redundancies
	Letter Styles and Envelope Addressing
	~~Guide Sheet~~
~~2:00 - 2:30~~	~~Computers in Business~~
~~2:30 - 2:45~~	~~Coffee Break~~
~~2:45 - 3:30~~ *2:00-3:00*	Time Management
	Dress For Success *lc*
	Self-Image
	On-The-Job Cases
	Minutes
	Stress
	Are You Resisting Progress?
Bold *3:00-3:15 Break*	Human Relations in the Office
~~3:30 - 3:45~~ *4:15-4:30*	*3:15-4:15 Computers in Business* Wrap Up
~~3:30 - 4:00~~ *4:30-5:00*	Evaluations and Questions

Thurs

From the Desk of
Mary Andrews
Human Resources and Development

A
T
C

Chris

I need an evaluation form for the June 29 seminar. Key the attached format, which I received at a seminar I attended recently.

Save it on disk as evalrept.evl

Due Thurs. p.m.

6. To what extent do you believe the program today is or will be beneficial to you?

   Low 1   2   3   4   5   6   7   8   9   10   High

7. Suggestions for improvements you may have on today's format, objectives, speakers, facility, arrangements, and so on, would be appreciated and used to improve future presentations.

   _____

   _____

   _____

Evaluation Report

Program _____ Date _____

DIRECTIONS: In each response below, please circle the number that best represents your opinion with regard to the question asked.

1. How would you rate the overall quality of the program?

   Low 1   2   3   4   5   6   7   8   9   10   High

2. How meaningful to you personally was the content of the program?

   Low 1   2   3   4   5   6   7   8   9   10   High

3. Were the objectives of each speaker clear?

   Low 1   2   3   4   5   6   7   8   9   10   High

4. Which part of the presentation do you believe will be the most helpful to you?

   _____

5. Would you like to have any one topic explored further? If so, which one?

   _____

   _____

   In what manner/method (workshop, speaker, etc.) would you like to see this done?

   _____

   _____

6. To what extent do you believe the program today is or will be beneficial to you?

   Low 1   2   3   4   5   6   7   8   9   10   High

7. Suggestions for improvements you may have on today's format, objectives, speakers, facility, arrangements, and so on, would be appreciated and used to improve future presentations.

   _____

   _____

   _____

INTEROFFICE MEMORANDUM

To: Mary Andrews
From: Mark Green
Date: January 24, ——
Subject: Leave Time

I want to take a leave of absence without pay from my job but I have accrued vacation time that I have not used. Can I take a leave of absence without pay without first using all of my vacation time? Please let me know as soon as possible.

st

Create envelope for confidential Gregs referenced manual

Chris—Send Mark the information about leave time, which is on the attached page—

—Please get it in the mail today (Tues.)

Mary Andrews

Allied Technology Corporation

**Human Resources and Development
Department Manager
402-555-4445**

Send this in Memo form to Mark Green today.   *SS*

An employee must use all *accrued* vacation time before taking a leave of absence unless circumstances allow the employee to use Family/Medical Leave (see final paragraph for description). Compenstaory time must also be taken or paid out before an employee begins a leave of absense withou pay.

As a regular employee, even if you are on corective probabion, you may be granted a leave of absence without pay with approval of your department and the Human Resources and Development Department. Such leave may be granted for aminimum of one day and maximum of one year. A laeve of absence ensure that you will have the same or similar job upon returning to the company.

Sick leave is not accrued *and vacation leave are* during a leave of absence. You may continue your insurance benefits during a leave of absence by paying the ntire premiun. You would need to contact the Benefitw Office for further information about continuing your insurance.

If your request for qa leave of absence is in regard to (1) your own serious health condition, (2) the serious heaelth condition of your child, parent or spouse, (3) maternal/paternal concern associated with the birth, adoption, or foster care of a child or (4) the death of a member of your immediate family, then you may qualify for laeve under the Family/Medical Leave policy. You do not have to use all acrued vacation leave prior to taking a leave under the Familyj/Medical Leave policy. Contact the company Human Resources Department for more information about type of leave.

¶ *If you have additional questions, call me at x4445.*

Tuesday

Mary Andrews

Allied
Technology
Corporation

Human Resources and Development
Department Manager
402-555-4445

RUSH

Chris--Make this into an attractive flyer. It will be offered Thursday March 16 and held in Conference Room B. The speaker will be Mr. Jack Ackerson of Business Skills, Inc., Des Moines, IA. Check on ZIP Code. Street address is 3345 South Main. Compose and send him a letter confirming the date and include a copy of the flyer. Use block letter format. Tell Mr. Ackerson that we will need to know what audiovisual equipment he will need and that we will need master copies of his handouts three weeks prior to the presentation. Also tell him that we will let him know how many will be attending when we have the registrations.   (Due today)

BUSINESS COMMUNICATIONS WORKSHOP
FOR OFFICE PERSONNEL
8 a.m. to 5 p.m.

Speaker: Jack Ackerson, Business Skills, Inc., Des Moines, IA

8:00 - 8:10		Introductory Comments
8:10 - 9:00 *9:10*		Punctuation Review
9:10 9:00 - 9:20 *10:10*		Skills Update
10:10 9:20 - 9:30 *10:30*		Break
10:30 9:30 - 9:50 *11:30*		Records Management *11:30 - 12:30 Lunch*
12:30 9:50 - 10:05 *1:30*		Office Teamwork
1:30 10:05 - 10:20 *2:30*		Coping with Stress
2:30 10:20 - 10:50 *3:30*		Prioritizing Work
3:30 10:50 - 11:00 *3:45*		Break
3:45 11:00 - 11:15 *4:30*		Business Image and Future Goals
~~11:15 - 11:40~~		~~Office Situation Case Studies~~
4:30 11:40 - 12:00 *5:00*		Discussion Period

~~Second Session would begin at 1:00 and finish at 5:00~~

Wednesday

Powerpoint

Mary Andrews

Allied
Technology
Corporation

Human Resources and Development
Department Manager
402-555-4445

I will be making a presentation on Thursday.

Prepare a transparency master for the "Work Attitudes" article, which is attached. List the main topics. Heading: Your Employer Has a Right to Expect the Following:

1. Capability

2. Dependability and promptness

3. Etc.

4.

5.

6.

7.

8.

9.

Rekey the article with corrections. Make all necessary changes (change he to he/she or him to him/her, etc.) Change single hyphens that represent a dash to two hyphens with no space before, after, or between. Be sure spacing is appropriate for easy reading.

—I will need this on Wednesday so we
can get copies made in time for
the presentation

(Students: Be sure to use large type for the transparency master and special fonts on the first letter of each item. Keep it all on one page.)

WORK ATTITUDES

Your employer has a right to expect the following:

1. Capability
   a. Do your present job to the best of your ability
   b. Keep busy
   c. You shouldn't need someone watching you all the time or telling you what to do next
   d. Do your work within the time allowed
   e. Do your work as well as anyone else - or better
   f. Don't ask others to help you with work that you are supposed to do on your own

2. Dependability and promptness
   a. Be on time
   b. Be at work every day - don't do what you "feel" like doing, but do what you're committed to do
   c. If you do miss work (for sickness, death in the family), call your employer

3. Cooperation
   a. Every worker does have his own work to do, but there is an implied understanding that each worker will help his fellow workers and employer if a necessity should arise
   b. When an unusual emergency arises, offer your services to help meet it
   c. The worker who does only what he is assigned and nothing more usually is given no more consideration than he has given in return

4. Initiative
   a. A full day's work for a full day's pay
   b. Search for additional work that can be done to prevent wasting idle periods
   c. Learn as much as possible about the task being done

5. Loyalty
   a. Speak well of your employers - don't tear them down
   b. No company is perfect - but speak of the favorable features - the people, the products, the plant
   c. If you can't say anything favorable about your company, you should leave

6. Honesty
   a. Stealing is wrong
   b. Taking home small items - paper, pencils, clips - is no less serious than taking larger items
   c. Large-scale pilfering can place a ruinous financial burden on a company
   d. Stealing of time by sneaking in late to work, extending coffee breaks, wasting time on the job, and leaving early are wrong
   e. Stealing of services by using the company phone for personal calls and submitting expense vouchers for personal entertainment is wrong
   f. Use honesty in speech and in written word
   g. Do not falsify reports

7. Acceptance of assignments and responsibilities
   a. Your employer has a right to change your assignments and responsibilities
   b. You should be ready and willing to assume any change within reason
   c. Certain assignments assure a smooth-running organization and eliminate arguments. If you are told to park in a certain area, park there. If you are given a certain phone, clothing rack, or storage bin, use it

8. Effort for improvement
   a. Your employer expects you to improve and to know your job thoroughly
   b. You should know something of the work done by others with whom you come into contact
   c. You should read the periodicals concerned with your trade

9. Acceptance of criticism
   a. Your employer has a right to criticize your work and your personal behavior while you are in your place of work; you may carefully and tactfully disagree
   b. An unacceptable worker is the one who feels he is never wrong. When criticized, he causes a disturbance by denying the allegation.

From the Desk of
Mary Andrews
Human Resources and Development

A
T
C

mailing labels merge

Find Customer List No. 34 in the <u>Employees'
Information Manual</u>. Enter the information
into a database and sort by ZIP Codes. Make a
set of mailing labels. Pull up the Customer
Appreciation Letter from the disk (custappr.ltr)
and send a copy to each person on Customer List
No. 34. You will need to use the Merge function.

— by Wednesday

From the Desk of
Mary Andrews
Human Resources and Development

A
T
C

Retrieve the article on "Successful Human
Relations at Work" from the disk (humrel.art).
It has a number of errors. Print a copy; mark the
errors, using correction symbols.

— I need this by Wednesday

M

Thursday

Confidential

From the Desk of
Mary Andrews
Human Resources and Development

A
T
C

Chris—

Prepare a memo with this information for Brad in Accounting. He needs it Thursday.

Mary

For Mary   **URGENT** ☐
Date 1-24   **Time** 2:15

WHILE YOU WERE OUT

Mr/Mrs/Ms Brad
Of Accounting
Phone X2998   **Ext.**

☒ **Phoned**   ☐ **Please Call**
☐ **Stopped By**   ☐ **Will Try Again**
☐ **Returned Call**   ☐ **Wishes a Meeting**

Message
Need SS#, Name, Salary, Deductions, Total Take-Home Pay before Taxes for Each HRD employee — Monthly and Yearly -Needs by Thurs.

rd

From the Desk of
Mary Andrews
Human Resources and Development

A
T
C

Chris—

SKIP

There are two articles on disk that I need to have summarized. They are: plntimpr.art and jobrevws.art. Key each summary onto a separate page and put on my desk before the end of the day.

Mary

From the Desk of
Mary Andrews
Human Resources and Development

A
T
C

Chris—

There are three items that I need transcribed from the tape on your desk. They are "Managing Your Weight Pays Off With Big Dividends," "Put On Your Thinking Cap," and "Professional Attire Pays Big Dividends in the Office Environment." Use plain white paper when you print the copies.

I need these today— Tuesday.

Mary

look online

Red Lion
Shilo
Double Tree

Still
need

Wednesday Assignment (January 25)

Thursday

Mary Andrews

*A*llied
*T*echnology
*C*orporation

Human Resources and Development
Department Manager
402-555-4445

I will be leaving from Omaha (Central Standard Time) for a conference in Los Angeles (Pacific Standard Time) from March 7–March 9.

Call our company travel agency and get the airline flight times and rates to Los Angeles on March 6 returning March 10.

(Students should call a local travel agency for this information or, if the students have access to the Internet, they may find the information there.)

Look online

Call the Los Angeles Downtown Corby Hotel and find out the following:

1) cost of 20 single sleeping rooms

2) cost for a conference room to seat 20 from 8 a.m. to 5 p.m. on March 7, 8, and 9 (Usually there is no charge for a conference room if a certain number of sleeping rooms are used.)

3) if non-smoking rooms are available

4) how long it takes to travel from airport to hotel

5) if there are facilities to accommodate the handicapped

6) time of check-in and time of check-out

7) cost of hotel garage services

(Students should refer to a travel journal for information about hotels and to find 800 numbers of larger hotels in the Los Angeles area. Students should each call a *different* hotel in the Los Angeles area. The instructor should give guidance on this.)

I need this information by Thurs.

Red Lion
Shilo
Double Tree

Still need memo

✓ *Wednesday*

Mary Andrews

Allied Technology Corporation

Human Resources and Development
Department Manager
402-555-4445

database

SEMINAR ATTENDEES

BILL ABOUD	3414 AVENUE TEN	KEARNEY	NE	68847
JIM ANDERSON	1689 CAMELOT WAY	KEARNEY	NE	68847
STEVE SAYER	316 N C AVENUE	BARTLEY	NE	69020
SHARI STONE	305 R STREET	BARTLEY	NE	69020
JACK TAYLOR	1978 N STREET	BARTLEY	NE	69020
GLEN JONES	3498 7TH STREET	BERTRAND	NE	68927
BETTY WOLFE	589 MEREDITH ROAD	BERTRAND	NE	68927
LINDA LUND	987 STABLE DRIVE	BARTLEY	NE	69020
F J PETRACEKE	821 BAY STREET	ELWOOD	NE	68937
LISA HARRISON	14 EAST MAIN	COZAD	NE	69130
CRAIG CRALL	978 HERITAGE STREET	COZAD	NE	69130
BILLIE PRICE	89 NOEL AVENUE	COZAD	NE	69130
JEREMY GEIG	3453 W 10TH	COZAD	NE	69130
JOHN MEYER	710 SOUTH STREET	EDISON	NE	68936
HENRY HASHI	2334 AMHERST STREET	MASCOT	NE	68967
SARAH MOSS	589 AVENUE S	EDISON	NE	68936
ELSIE STROH	908 B STREET	EDISON	NE	68936

Chris—

Here is the list of seminar attendees. Enter the names into the database (~~use all Caps~~ and name the file "sematend.lst"). We will need to use them to send out thank-you letters and certificates later this week. Be sure to alphabetize them.

I need this done today.

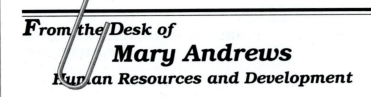

From the Desk of
Mary Andrews
Human Resources and Development

Here is an article on Supervisor's Responsibilities, which I plan to use as a handout. Make changes as indicated and rekey. Also, set up the material for transparencies—place each section on a separate transparency master. Be sure to make them as attractive as possible. Make the print large enough to see from the back of a large room.

Chris—I need this Thurs.

... and center title

... GANIZATION ↙

... passing along

... sing the buck."

... ng superiors

... d to cooperate with

... sors for the good

... ts.

... the results.

4. Evaluating employees periodically and recommending promotions, salary adjustments, transfers, and dismissals.

5. Delegating authority and responsibility in order to develop understudies.

6. Developing harmony, cooperation, and teamwork.

7. Building and maintaining employee morale and handling grievances promptly and fairly.

8. Maintaining discipline and controlling absenteeism and tardiness.

9. Taking a personal interest in subordinates without showing partiality.

10. Using courtesy, tact, and consideration in treating subordinates as human beings.

↰ *Use bullets instead of numbers on all these items and on the transparency masters*

Thurs
Retype + make powerpoint

Change title to initial caps and bold—increase size and center title

SUPERVISOR'S RESPONSIBILITIES TO OTHERS IN THE BUSINESS ORGANIZATION

Upward responsibilities to higher management: *Bold*

Summarize bullet items

1. Ascertaining and carrying out what management wants done.

2. Keeping superiors informed of what is being done in the department and passing along ideas for improvement.

3. Accepting full responsibility for the work in the department without "passing the buck."

4. Referring matters requiring superiors' attention promptly without bothering superiors unnecessarily.

5. Interpreting the employees' needs to management, and vice versa.

Horizontal responsibilities to peers: *Bold*

1. Cooperating with peers in the same manner that subordinates are expected to cooperate with one another.

2. Helping coordinate the work of the department with that of other supervisors for the good of the firm.

3. Permitting interchange and promotion of good workers among departments.

Downward responsibilities to subordinates: *Bold*

1. Aiding in selection and orientation of new workers.

2. Training and counseling subordinates to assume greater responsibilities.

3. Assisting employees to know what to do and how to do it and checking the results.

4. Evaluating employees periodically and recommending promotions, salary adjustments, transfers, and dismissals.

5. Delegating authority and responsibility in order to develop understudies.

6. Developing harmony, cooperation, and teamwork.

7. Building and maintaining employee morale and handling grievances promptly and fairly.

8. Maintaining discipline and controlling absenteeism and tardiness.

9. Taking a personal interest in subordinates without showing partiality.

10. Using courtesy, tact, and consideration in treating subordinates as human beings.

Use bullets instead of numbers on all these items and on the transparency masters

Wednesday

Mary Andrews

Allied
Technology
Corporation

Human Resources and Development
Department Manager
402-555-4445

RUSH

Chris—

Dr. Barnes has consented to do this seminar next month for those individuals who may have missed her previous course. Key the following memo and send it to all the department managers, along with the schedule. Can you do it now?

Attached is information to the support staff regarding a refresher course in business communication skills, which the firm is offering.

It is believed that the course is necessary and will result in considerable improvement in the communications emanating from this office.

The Management Committee believes that all administrative assistants should attend and participate in <u>all sessions</u>. The refresher course is not an inexpensive activity, and we wish to get the greatest value from it. You, therefore, are requested to impress upon your administrative assistant the importance of his/her faithful attendance. You are further requested <u>not to interfere</u> with your administrative assistant's attendance except in the most extreme emergency.

Please feel free to attend any or all of the sessions presented.

Bold—initial caps only

BUSINESS COMMUNICATIONS SKILLS REFRESHER COURSE FOR ADMINISTRATIVE ASSISTANTS AND OFFICE PERSONNEL

Have you forgotten when to use a singular verb and when to use a plural verb? Are you hesitant about where to place your commas? Do number rules cause you to search frantically through your <u>Office Handbook</u> for correct usage? Are you uncertain about the correct rules for possessive forms? ~~Have basic filing rules slipped away from recall?~~ *Do you have difficulty managing your records?*

Here's a chance to improve your professional skills. Join the Brown Bag Lunch Group for some helpful review tips on numerous problem areas of business communications.

This course will consist of 8 meetings, each 60 minutes in length. There will be a review of the major problem areas in business communication. The course will be offered on Tuesdays and Thursdays, ~~April 12 through May 5~~ *February 7 through March 2*, at 11:30 to 12:30 or 12:30 to 1:30. The following topics will be covered: *a.m.* *p.m.* *p.m.* *in Conference Room 14.*

Session No.	1	Punctuation
"	2	Hyphenation and Word Division
"	3	Capitalization and Number Usage
"	4	Abbreviations, Contractions, Plurals, and Possessives
"	5	Words Misused and Confused; Spelling Rules
"	6	Grammar and Usage; ~~Filing Rules~~ *Records Management*
"	7	Business Letters, Memorandums, Reports, Minutes
"	8	Proofreading, Editing, Word Processing

and Manuscripts

Friday

From the Desk of
Mary Andrews
Human Resources and Development

Chris—

Here are some items for the next newsletter. (Save the item about computers and electrical storms until later in the spring but go ahead and set it in columns now so it is ready in the spring—do it on a separate page.) Set up the rest of the material in columns and with proper titles and send to the printing office. They need it this Fri.

AL⋯ ⋯OYEES

⋯ion during the

p⋯st⋯
Joy⋯
Elle⋯
Pau⋯
Lin⋯
Kris⋯
Sha⋯
Ricl⋯
Den⋯

NE⋯

sess⋯
exte⋯
are⋯

RE⋯

the⋯
tion⋯

PAF⋯

rela⋯
und⋯
spac⋯

14. Six-week
conditioning,
Class schedules

8 at 10 a.m. in
⋯nology Corpora-

⋯ are having
⋯ has been
⋯ough parking
⋯d it is hoped that
a satisfactory solution will soon be presented to the employees. In the meantime, First State Bank on the corner of State and Maple Streets has offered the use of its parking lot to our employees. The parking lot maintenance will take about three months to complete if the weather cooperates.

UNPLUG YOUR COMPUTER DURING STORMS

Many Allied Technology Corporation personnel have home computers. Personal computer users need to be mindful of the weather during thunderstorm season. The computer should be turned off during an electrical storm. Otherwise, lightning can race through telephone wires and enter the computer through its modem.

In some cases, only the modem will be damaged, but the entire computer could be lost. Also, if lightning strikes near your home, it can cause power surges through your electrical outlets, delivering 20,000 volts of electricity to your computer.

Publisher Newsletter   *Friday*

ALLIED TECHNOLOGY CORPORATION WELCOMES NEW EMPLOYEES

The following employees have joined Allied Technology Corporation during the past quarter. We welcome them to our company.

Joyce Ash	Facilities Management	x3456
Ellen Bright	Library Resource Center	x2489
Paul Johnson	Printing Services	x4976
Linda Martin	Accounting Department	x2221
Kristin Osburn	Landscape Services	x9344
Sharon West	Health Center	x9009
Hector Garcia	Archives Center	x1469
Denise Miller	Records Management	x8965

NEW FITNESS CLASSES BEGIN FEBRUARY 14

Session III of the Winter Fitness Class Schedule begins February 14. Six-week sessions are scheduled in areas including step, step forward, total body conditioning, extended step, power step, progressive/low impact, and Spanish combo. Class schedules are available in the Health Center. For more information, call x9009.

RETIREMENT RECEPTION PLANNED

A retirement reception will be held for Jack Simpson on February 8 at 10 a.m. in the Atrium. Simpson is retiring after ten years of service to Allied Technology Corporation, where he worked in the Accounting Department.

PARKING PROBLEMS AND SOLUTIONS

The administration is continuing work on the problems employees are having related to parking. Since the Allied Technology Corporation parking lot has been undergoing maintenance, it has become increasingly difficult to find enough parking spaces within walking distance. Several suggestions have been made and it is hoped that a satisfactory solution will soon be presented to the employees. In the meantime, First State Bank on the corner of State and Maple Streets has offered the use of its parking lot to our employees. The parking lot maintenance will take about three months to complete if the weather cooperates.

UNPLUG YOUR COMPUTER DURING STORMS

Many Allied Technology Corporation personnel have home computers. Personal computer users need to be mindful of the weather during thunderstorm season. The computer should be turned off during an electrical storm. Otherwise, lightning can race through telephone wires and enter the computer through its modem.

In some cases, only the modem will be damaged, but the entire computer could be lost. Also, if lightning strikes near your home, it can cause power surges through your electrical outlets, delivering 20,000 volts of electricity to your computer.

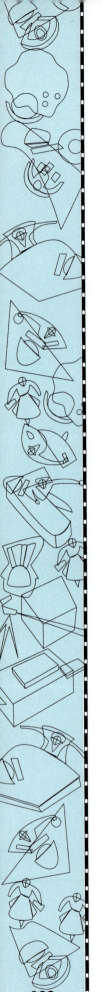

During an electrical storm, follow these steps:

• Stop working and unplug your PC if the weather is severe; if you have a modem attached, remove the phone cord.

• Change your surge protector every three or four years. The devices, particularly less expensive models, can wear out over time.

• Remember to unplug your PC before leaving for trips or vacations, even if you have a surge protector.

TELECOMMUTING NOT GAINING FAST

Allied Technology Corporation is one of the few companies that allow some office employees to engage in telecommuting. Most of the employees and employers who are involved in this new method of working at home believe that it benefits both the company and the individual. However, not all companies are in agreement about this new work plan.

Telecommuting remains slow to catch on in the American work force, a new survey indicates. Less than 1 percent of the staff at organizations that allow employees to work at home actually are taking advantage of the option.

The nationwide study, based on a poll of 155 employers, found that skeptical middle managers are the main obstacle preventing the more widespread practice of telecommuting.

While other studies also have found that only a tiny percentage of office workers do their jobs from home, the most surprising fact was that the number remained low even at organizations that, at least on paper, endorse telecommuting.

More than two-thirds of these employers also contributed to the cost of telecommuting by paying for computers, telephone service, and office supplies.

HEALTH CENTER OFFERS WEIGHT CONTROL CLASSES

Promoting gradual and permanent weight loss is what the Health Center's "Active Way to Weight Control" program is all about.

Participants attend ten one-hour sessions over ten weeks. At each session, there will be an opportunity to weigh in, followed by an educational presentation and open discussion. Topics include exercise, self-esteem/body image, nutrition, fad diets, stress, and more.

To register, you must have a medical evaluation prior to acceptance in the program. Bring a written statement from your personal physician to the first class.

Two class times are offered on Tuesdays beginning February 7. Class times are from 11:50 a.m. to 12:50 p.m. or from 3:30 to 4:30 p.m. The cost of $25 covers materials used in the course.

You must receive written permission from your department manager to attend the 3:30 p.m. session. To register, call the Health Center at x9009 by February 1.

From the Desk of
Mary Andrews
Human Resources and Development

ATC

Chris—Retrieve the letter on Seminar Pay (sempay.ltr) from the disk. Send a copy to Dr. Virginia Long, Business Education, 3425 Ellery Hall, Emerson College, Cheyenne, WY 82001. Use the following figures:

35 admin. assist. @ $65 =
Meals ($40 per day) x 2 = $80
Air fare ($495) = 495
Hotel ($95 per day) x 2 =

Calculate the check total.
Mail this today.

Wednesday

From the Desk of
Mary Andrews
Human Resources and Development

ATC

Chris—The printing office called and said they are really short on items for the newsletter. Retrieve the following items from the disk, put them together into column form, and send them along with the other newsletter materials I asked you to do earlier. Be sure they get them by Friday. Put them in a large manila envelope and address them to John in Printing.

Put in newsletter Friday

Advertising Tips (advtips.art)
Lost Car Phone Can Be Costly (carphone.art)
The Telephone is a Valuable Asset if Used Correctly (telephon.art)
Job Sharing—Two People in One Job! Will It Work? (jobshare.art)
OCR Scanning Saves Time and Money (OCR.art)
How Well Do You Know Your Rights? (knowrigh.art)

n.

Wednesday

Mary Andrews

Allied Technology Corporation

Human Resources and Development Department Manager
402-555-4445

Wed—Chris—

I slipped up on this— We need to find out from each department manager how many service awards we need for five, ten, fifteen, twenty, and twenty-five years of service. We need the name and number of years for each person. The Awards Ceremony will be Friday, March 10, at noon in the Centennial Room. (We will need to see the menus available for that day.)

If I recall correctly, last year we had 75 people attend. The ceremony lasted until 2:30 p.m. We used yellow napkins and white table cloths. We had carnation flower arrangements on the tables. We ordered the awards from Outstanding Awards Company on Market Street. Each person being recognized received a separate invitation to the ceremony. Each department manager presented the awards to his/ her employees. There was also a program for the event, which was printed in-house; we will want this done again, and you may also be able to confirm some of the details from last year's event by looking at the old program.

Take care of all the arrangements immediately— and make a list of what you have done so that I can be sure we haven't overlooked anything. Let me see any memos or other items that you have sent, too.

email list of things to that need to be done

For	Mary	URGENT [X]
Date	1-25	Time 8:15

WHILE YOU WERE OUT

Mr/Mrs/Ms Charlotte Marks
Of Purchasing
Phone _____ Ext. 7887

[X] Phoned   [ ] Please Call
[ ] Stopped By   [ ] Will Try Again
[ ] Returned Call   [ ] Wishes a Meeting

Message
We need to order the service awards at least a month before the ceremony.

rd

From the Desk of
Mary Andrews
Human Resources and Development

A
T
C

Chris—

I need to have the attached six items keyed into the computer so that we can retrieve them quickly.

—Due on Thursday

(rm.ltr)

SKIP
111-117

subject) to be held on
be notified of the

and they are interested

your personal travel
honorarium amount of
that you actually

Mary Andrews, Manager
Human Resources and Development Department

xx

Enclosure: Memorandum of Agreement

c (person in charge of seminar at seminar location)

(date)

(inside address)

(File name = confirm.ltr)

(salutation)

Please accept this letter as a confirmation of your workshop on (subject) to be held on (date), ——, with the Allied Technology Corporation. You will be notified of the exact location at a later date.

The arrangements involved in this workshop are as follows:

1. The presentation will be from (   ) a.m. to (   ) p.m.

2. There will be approximately (   ) people in attendance and they are interested in dealing with the aspects of (   ).

I am enclosing a memorandum of agreement, which would cover your personal travel expenses and expenses for any materials you might have plus an honorarium amount of $(   ). The honorarium would cover the time that you actually conduct the workshop and preparation time that you require.

If you have any questions, feel free to call me at 402-555-4445.

Sincerely

Mary Andrews, Manager
Human Resources and Development Department

xx

Enclosure: Memorandum of Agreement

c (person in charge of seminar at seminar location)

(date)

(inside address)

(File name = semarrg.ltr)

(salutation)

Thank you for your (date) letter and seminar agenda. Enclosed is an updated list of attendees. If there are any changes after this, I will inform you by (   ). We will have a carousel projector available.

All necessary arrangements for your stay have been made at the Best City Hotel; the billing will be made to our company. They have excellent dining and recreational facilities as well as outstanding service. I am also enclosing two maps of Omaha and have marked the Best City Hotel and the Allied Technology Corporation. I hope these will be of help to you.

We are looking forward to your visit; the seminar program looks exciting. We are pleased with your choice of topics. Call me at 402-555-4445 if you have any questions.

Sincerely

Mary Andrews, Manager
Human Resources and Development Department

xx

Enclosures: Updated list of attendees
             Maps of Omaha

(Students: Retrieve the two Omaha maps from the World Wide Web. One should be of the downtown area and one should be of the airport area.)

Seminar/Workshop Agreement

The **Allied Technology Corporation** agrees to cover the following expense

items for (name of presenter)

for presentation of workshop/seminar entitled

(name of workshop)

(File name = semagree.doc)

on (date/s).

( ) employees @ $( )	$ ( )
Meals ($) per day	( )
Air (or mileage @ $( ) per mile)	( )
Hotel ($) per day	( )
Supplies ($)	( )
Honorarium ($) per day	( )
Total	$ ( )

_____   _____
(Signature of Allied Technology Corporation Manager)   (Date)

_____   _____
(Signature of person contracting for the presentation)   (Date)

(date)

(inside address)

(File name = semsched.ltr)

(salutation)

There has been an overwhelming response to the administrative assistant seminars being offered on (date). Attached is a tentative list of attendees. It appears that there will be ( ) employees (per day) present. There may be some additional changes, but I will keep you informed.

The seminar will be held in the large training center, which is equipped with an overhead projector and large screen. Please plan one extra folder for the administrative assistant to our president and chief executive officer. It appears now that her schedule will not permit her to attend. Let me know if you need additional supplies.

A schedule that usually works well is to have a morning break at 10:15 a.m., lunch from 11:45 a.m. to 12:45 p.m., and an afternoon break at 2:15 p.m. Is this agreeable with you?

Based on the tentative attached list, our reimbursement to you would be:

( ) employees @ $( )	$ ( )	
Meals ($) per day	( )	
Air (or mileage @ $( ) per mile)	( )	
Hotel ($) per day	( )	
Supplies ($)	( )	

Reservations have been made for you at the Best City Hotel for (dates). This will be billed directly to Allied Technology Corporation. Please send me an outline of any "introductory" information you want sent to the administrative assistants prior to the seminar.

If you have any questions regarding the above, call me at 402-555-4445. I'm looking forward to meeting you!

Sincerely

Mary Andrews, Manager
Human Resources and Development Department

xx

Attachment: Registration List

(date)

(inside address)   *(File name = marysfee.ltr)*

(salutation)

It would be a pleasure to return to your city to do a seminar on what is new in office communications, plus a thorough review of punctuation and filing rules. There seems to be a real demand for this type of refresher course in many offices today.

The fees for the two-day seminar (dates) would be as follows:

( ) employees @ $( )	$ ( )
Meals ($) per day	( )
Air (or mileage @ $( ) per mile)	( )
Hotel ($) per day	( )
Supplies ($)	( )
Honorarium ($) per day	( )

It is my understanding that your Training Center will be used for the seminar and that an overhead projector and large screen will be available for my use. The seminar hours will be 9 a.m. until 4 p.m. with two refreshment breaks and an hour noon break. I will send the materials for my handouts three weeks before the presentation date.

I look forward to meeting you and working with your administrative assistants and office personnel.

Sincerely

Mary Andrews, Manager
Human Resources and Development Department

xx

SKIP

(date)

(inside address)

(File name = maryssem.ltr)

(salutation)

Enclosed is the agenda that I plan to use at the administrative assistant seminar on (date). I am happy to hear that you are having a good response.

It sounds as if you have taken care of all the necessary arrangements. Yes, I would enjoy having dinner with you and the other administrative assistants on (   ) evening. I understand that you have an active Professional Secretaries International Association in (city), and I would like to hear more about it.

I will probably not arrive in (city) until late (   ) evening. Since I will have a number of items to bring with me, I plan to drive my rental car to your office and will be there by 8:15 a.m. (   ) morning. Please send directions of the route between the hotel and your office.

I am looking forward to spending two pleasant and productive days in your city.

Sincerely

Mary Andrews, Manager
Human Resources and Development Department

xx

Enclosure: Agenda

ask to see Kay Friday

Mary Andrews

Allied Technology Corporation

Human Resources and Development
Department Manager
402-555-4445

Thursday

By Friday--Enter these petty cash expenses into a spreadsheet so I can see if we are keeping within our budget.

Week of December 19-23:
12/19 Received cash of $90
Paid Out: transparencies, $16.98 on 12/20; highlight pens, $14.99 on 12/21; notebooks, $7.98 on 12/22; tea bags, $3.55, and creamer, $3.57 on 12/23

Week of December 27-30:
12/27 Received cash of $90
Paid Out: donation to charity, $25 on 12/27; snacks for office, $23.95 on 12/27; map, $5.50 on 12/28; stapler, $6.60 on 12/28; paper clips, $3.58 on 12/29; plastic disk sleeves, $8.45 on 12/30

Week of January 3-6:
1/3 Received cash of $90
Paid Out: $45.12 on 1/3 for plastic cups, plates, napkins; $12.55 on 1/3 for pencils; $4.55 on 1/4 for scissors; $3.98 on 1/5 for staple remover; $16.45 on 1/6 for ZIP Code book

Week of January 9-13:
Received cash of $90 on 1/9
Paid Out: $23 on 1/9 for ad for newspaper; $10.35 on 1/10 for messenger service; $15.65 on 1/11 for pens; $25 on 1/12 for donation to charity; $15.25 for snacks for office on 1/13

Week of January 16-20:
Received cash of $90 on 1/16
Paid Out: $25 on 1/16 for donation to charity; $8.48 for office snacks on 1/17; $12.19 for notepads on 1/18; on 1/19, $5.50 for envelopes; and $4.95 for coffee on 1/20

Chart   Friday

$\begin{matrix} A \\ T \\ C \end{matrix}$ INTEROFFICE MEMORANDUM

To: Mary Andrews, HRD
From: Cindy Lindley, Accounting
Date: January 25, ——
Subject: Hours of Temporary Workers in HRD

Please send me a list of your temporary workers in HRD, the regular hours worked, and the overtime hours worked for the week of January 16 to 20. What is the total number of hours for each and the gross earnings for each?

mm

Chris—Can you figure this for Cindy and send it to her by Friday? We have eight temporary people and they each get $6.40 per hour. Overtime is time-and-a-half. Put the information into chart form. Use a spreadsheet.

Name	Hours Worked	Regular Earnings	Overtime Earnings	Total Gross Earnings
John Apple	25			
Tang Che	33			
Jack Cliff	45			
Frank Duff	12 1/2			
Georgia Huf	36 3/4			
Heather Nes	53			
Sally Sprig	15			
Jenny Moss	51 1/2			

Total Gross Earnings

thursday

Mary Andrews

Allied
Technology
Corporation

Human Resources and Development
Department Manager
402-555-4445

Chris--The Legal Department sent me this list. They need
the following customer folders from the file. You will
need to alphabetize the list before you go to the file
drawers to retrieve the files tomorrow (Thursday). I
have underlined the surnames to use for the first
indexing unit.

Also, retrieve the Customer Appreciation Letter
(custappr.ltr) from the disk and send a copy to Alicia
Diaz, 98 Maple Drive, Omaha, NE 68144 and to Kim Barnes,
1531 Hillsdale Park, Lincoln, NE 68502. (Please send the
letters no later than tomorrow.)

John <u>Wozniak</u>
Gene R. <u>Wrigglesworth</u>
Denhy Tao-Yuan <u>Wu</u>   *Skip?*
Wu <u>Shikuei</u>
Violet <u>Wuerfel</u>
Anna Belle <u>Werth</u>
Letty <u>Wunglueck</u>
Mike <u>Jaeger</u>
M. <u>Yager</u>
Edward <u>Zarafonetis</u>
Roger <u>Zauel</u>
Jung Suk <u>Youn</u>
Robert <u>Young</u>
Peter <u>Yates</u>
Toshibisa <u>Yotsuyanagi</u>
V.J. <u>Wrobleski</u>
Ching-Jung <u>Wu</u>
Elfreda <u>Wrathell</u>
Sharon <u>Wroblewski</u>
Wong Tong <u>Yong</u>
Gregory <u>Yeatts</u>
Judy <u>Jong</u>
Artee <u>Younge</u>

Wednesday   Excel

Mary Andrews

Allied
Technology
Corporation

Human Resources and Development
Department Manager
402-555-4445

Cindy Lindley is to make a presentation to a group this afternoon. She needs help with a graphic master for the following information. Can you prepare one and deliver it to her office by noon? Use your best judgment on what kind of a graphic would be the most effective.

Mary

Office Expenses for December

Stationery	$560
Pens, pencils, miscellaneous	230
Envelopes (all sizes)	450
Laser toner	350
Paper clips, map pins, etc.	60
Computer disks	250
Subscriptions	150
Electric pencil sharpener	30
Stapler	20
Notepads	240

From the Desk of
Mary Andrews
Human Resources and Development

A
T
C

Chris—

Today (Wednesday) write a letter for me to Barry Smith at our Denver branch office (see the <u>Employees' Information Manual</u> for the address—use Dear Barry for the salutation) asking him to send me the following information:

Wednesday

1) Number of employees in his branch office

2) Number of males and number of females in the Denver branch office

3) Average salary of the men and average salary of the women in his branch office

4) Average number of years the men have worked in his branch office

5) Average number of years the women have worked in his branch office

Ask him to fax the information to me by Friday, if possible.

~~A~~ndrews
~~…~~nd Development

A
T
C

Print & mark up

We have a disk copy of "Meeting Guidelines and Parliamentary Procedure" (meetguid.doc), which needs a lot of corrections. Try to do it today so I can go over it with some company officials on Thursday. A copy is attached.

Correct all errors, such as typos, words omitted, etc., which I haven't marked. Pull up a copy from the disk and make all the necessary changes. Use pre-set tabs to indent paragraphs appropriately. Be sure to change "he" and "him" to "he/she" and "him/her" whenever that occurs. Also, watch for consistency in numbers, etc. Read the article carefully to be sure it makes sense. Print a corrected copy for me.

Meeting Guidelines
And Parlimentary Procedure

Parliamentary procecure is one of the most effective means by which individuals can take orderly acton as a group. One can give full consideration to to any matter of of common interest, encourage common-sense minority discussion on each question, then act according to the will of the majority--all with a minimum wast of time.

There are some sound reasons why one should aquire a good working knowledge of parliamentary procedure.

Before the Meeting

The chairperson should check the arrangement ofchairs and tables before the meeting starts, striving for informality and friendliness. Their should be a table fro the chairperson and for the secretary so the to can work closely together. Check on attendants of each person who is scheduled to give report.

Order of Business

1.   Call the meeting to order

2.   roll call

3.   Minutes of the previous meeting

3.   Reports of the officers

   a. president

   b. vice president

   c. Treasurer

   d. secretary

5.   Standing Committee Reports

6.   Special committee reports

7.   Unfinished business

8.   Postponed Business

9.   New business

10. Adjournment

<u>What the Minutes Includes</u>

The minutes should contain the following information:

1.   Kind of meeting, regular or special

2.   Name of the organiation

3.   Date and place of meeting

4.   Presense of regular president and secretary or names of substitutes

5.   Approval of previous mimutes

7.   All reports and action taken

7   All main motions carried or lost (omit those withdrawn)

8.   All ohter motions caried and which contain imformation needed future meeting

9.   Adjournment.

10. Signature

<u>Report of the Treasurer</u>

When a treasurer's report is made from meeting to meeting, it should be *received*. This means the report was heard; it does not give official approval by the group. The treasuere's report should never be *accepted* or *approved* unless the books has been audited. A treasurer's report is audited when two or more members are requested to check all bills received and paid. All Figures are checked. The auditors report that the books "are in good order and found correct." The auditors report then is *approved* or *accepted* by the group.

Voting Terminology

MAJORITY--more than half the votes *cast*; used in elections and on most motions. Note that a majority does not mean more than half of the members present; but of the votes *cast*, since some may not care to vote.

TWO-THIRDS--2/3 of the votes *cast*; used with motions only.

PLURALITY--more than any other candidate; used only in elections when the assembly desires to save time. In electing a committee of three, the three nominees with the greatest number of votes will be considered elect.

GENERAL CONSENT--This is a a shortcut in voting. It permits the assembly to take action without going through the process of a regular vote.

This method should be used with all motions on which there seems to be a general agreement among the members. It is an excellent time-saver and should be used at every opportunity. For example, "If there are no objections, we will vote by ballot; (pause) No objecions? We will vote by ballot." In this way a group may quickly express there opinion. Now is someone objects, the Chair must put the motion to a regular vote. "All those in favor of voting by ballot say 'Aye' etc. . ."

The following are the methods of voting:

Acclamation or voice--"Aye"--"No"

Show of hands

Rising

secret ballot

Secret roll call ballot (sing names)

Roll call vote (members respond when name is called).

When the word "division" is stated by a member, he or she is requesting that another vote be taken on a motion. Generally this is done whenever a vote by acclamation fails to show clearly whether the vote was affirmative or negative. The method of voting used after division is called should be one that can observed by all, such as rasigin the hand or rising.

The chairperson should strive to be as impartial as possible, voting only if it will change the result. The Chair may vot to *break a tie* and cause the motion to carry, or vote to *make a tie* and cause the motion to lose

When the vote is public (by acclamation, rising, etc.), the chairperson should vote, if the Chair chooses to do so, *after* the assembly has voted and after the results have ben made known to the chair.

When the vote is secret (by ballot), the Chair should vote at the time that the assembly votes, and then cannot vote again to change the result.

The secretary has the write to vote at any and all times. The performance of secretarial duties shall not prevent the exercise of this right.

Motions

A motion is a REQUEST that some thing be done for that something is the opinion or wish of the assembly. There are various types of motions:

A MAIN MOTION introduces an action to the assembly for it's consideration. Only one main motion should be placed before the assembly at on time. It is always debatable and amendable, and it ranks below all other motions.

A main motion is any motion that brings on item of business before the assembly. It requires the *action* of the theassembly.

A PRIVILEGED MOTION refers two the action of the assembly as a whol; e.g., take a recess, adjourn, ect

A SUBSIDIARY MOTION is a motion applied to other motions, usually the main motion; to alter, postpone, to temporarily dispose of them.

An INCIDENTAL MOTION is use in conducting business and must be disposed of before action is taken on the motion out of which it arises. Example: motion to closee nominations, point of order, method of voting

RENEWAL MOTION is one that brings back to the floor a motion that one has been considered, but which the assembly wishes too consider again. Example: To reconsider, to take from table, to discharge an committee.

IF A MOTION IS pending, It means that the motion is on the floor but, as yet, not disposed of. Several motions may be on the floor at one time provided they were made in order of ascending rank. When several motions are pending the one *made last* is always disposed of *first* .

Changing a Motion

The motion to amend is a subsidiary motion and is always applied to another motion, usually the main motion. The motion to amend may be applied in several ways: to add; to insert; to strike out; to strike out and insert. Example: Main motion--to purchase a computer. While this motion is being discussed, an amendment is made to add the word, "and a printer."

Whenever possible, the chair should ask the maker of the main motion to change it to include the amendment. It is done this way: "Sally, would you agree to include this amendment in your motion, to add the words, 'and a printer?" If Sally agrees, and the assembly does not object, the motion is ammended If any member objects, the amendment must be second, be opened to discussion, or be amended and voted on the same as any motion.

Always vote on the amendment *before* you vote on the motion to which the amendment is applied. The discussion of an amendment should always be about the amendment itself and not about the main motion. An amendment should never insert the word, "not", in a motion to which it is applied, since that would be the same as a negative vote

A motion may be amended be several times in sucession; however only two amendments can be applied to a motion at one time: a primary amendment and a secondary amendment. The secondary amendment mujst always apply directly to the promary and not skip back to the main motion. Example: Main motion--*to purchase a table*; Primary amendment--to insert "*oak*" before table; Secondary amendment--to insert "*blond*" before oak

Friday

Mary Andrews

Allied Technology Corporation

**Human Resources and Development
Department Manager
402-555-4445**

---

p. 76

Chris,

Here is the information on preferred vacation times that the employees
in our department have requested. Please complete the chart I asked
you to create on Monday. I asked for it on Friday, but if you can finish it
sooner, that would be great! Be sure to complete Vacation Request forms,
also. Use HRD for the Department name; leave the "As Of" box blank.
Leave the bottom half of the form blank.

Mary

July 10 to 21	James Lamberty
August 7 to 11	Sally Jones
September 11 to 15	Henry Smythe
October 9 to 20	Chris Downing
December 11 to 22	Dwight Harms
November 6 to 10	Sally Jones
September 18 to 29	Mary Pare
August 21 to 25	Henry Smythe
August 21 to 25	E.F. Rodriguez
July 24 to 28	Henry Smythe
August 7 to 25	John E. Ross
December 18 to 22	E.F. Rodriguez
November 6 to 10	E.F. Rodriguez
December 18 to 22	James Lamberty

Thursday Assignment (January 26)

From the Desk of
Mary Andrews
Human Resources and Development

A T C

Chris—I asked Dr. Holmes to evaluate our Administrative Assistant tests. Key this information in a letter form and send it to the branch managers. Use Ms. or Mr. before the names in the addresses and in the salutation.

Try to make the table more attractive. The letter will probably be two pages. Use the names of the managers in the second-page heading (again using the Mr. or Ms.)

I need this today (Thurs.)

2 page letter

Nebraska,
e her

e a good
a number of
ts.

gestion would
est could be
art could still
ime to look up
s should have
e assistant may
fore, it seems
d part of the

llege business
his university,
ts.

s after working
heir abilities,
can be

ler in Which I
uld Hire Student

A	2	2	3
A	7	6	2
A	7	8	1
B+	4	6	-
B+	3	5	7
B+	9	5	-
B+	6	7	4
B+	7	6	8
B+	7	7	9
B	7	6	5
B	9	6	6

Dr. Diana Holmes, College of Continuing Studies, University of Nebraska, Lincoln, evaluated our Administrative Assistant test. Following are her comments:

Proofreading: This test seems to be quite complete and should give a good indication of the proofreading skills of your applicants. It includes a number of errors that should be detected by most good administrative assistants.

Word Choice: This test seems to be quite comprehensive. My suggestion would be to break it into two separate parts since results of the present test could be misleading. A person who does not score well on the vocabulary part could still make an excellent administrative assistant if he/she took the extra time to look up the words that are unfamiliar. However, all administrative assistants should have good grammar skills. If this skill is not automatic, an administrative assistant may often make errors without even realizing there is a problem. Therefore, it seems that it is more important that the applicant score well on the second part of the test.

Following are the results of your test when given to a group of college business students. Most of the students are in their first or second year at this university, and most of them work as full- or part-time administrative assistants.

I have also indicated the order in which I would hire these students after working with them in a classroom situation for a few weeks and realizing their abilities, potential, and dedication to hard work. As you can see, test scores can be somewhat deceiving.

Grade in Class	No. Missed on Proofreading	Average No. Missed Per Page on Word Choice	Order in Which I Would Hire Student
A	2	2	3
A	7	6	2
A	7	8	1
B+	4	6	-
B+	3	5	7
B+	9	5	-
B+	6	7	4
B+	7	6	8
B+	7	7	9
B	7	6	5
B	9	6	6

fix table

2nd page
1 line header

odd + even

Holmes   *page #*   *Date*

Mary Andrews

Allied Technology Corporation

**Human Resources and Development
Department Manager
402-555-4445**

*Thursday—Send a letter to Dr. Margaret Barnes, College of
Continuing Studies, University of Nebraska—Lincoln, 93 and Spring,
Lincoln, NE 68588-0515. The enclosures are the items you keyed
yesterday (Wed.). Single space the body and double space between
paragraphs. Please send this out today.*

Dear Dr. Barnes

I thought that you would like to know that the course you
will be teaching in our confrence room has generated a great
deal of conversation and everything that I have heard has been
positive. I think you are going to find a group of very
receptive students.

The text has been ordered and should arrive next week. I
have enclosed a copy of a memo that has been sent to our
administrative assistants and a second memo that has been sent
to the department managers.

Did you tell me that you needed an overhead projector and
a screen? We have both. Please give me a call if you need
these visual aids or have any questions.

We are looking forward to the course.

Sincerely --(add usual closing)

2 spaces   */Seminar Program*

Enclosures: Copy of Memo to Administrative Assistants
               Copy of Memo to Department Managers

*There is an overhead projector and a screen in the conference room. Let me
know if you need anything else.*

SKIP

Bold and increase size of heading →

How to Reduce Health Problems Resulting from Computer Use

There is a lot of information in newspapers and magazines about the health hazards of computer use. Most of this information has not been carefully researched and the risks actually proven. However, it is smart for people to be cautious and to use reasonable preventive measures if their job involves large amounts of time in front of a computer. Following are some suggestions for reducing health hazards for computer users:

• A wrist pad elevates your wrists to help eliminate the risk of carpal tunnel syndrome. This item is available from any software dealer.

• A glare/radiation screen can help reduce radiation emitting from your monitor. The screen should be properly grounded and composed of metal mesh or metalized plastic. Nylon mesh screens with carbon coating lose their protection over time. You should be 28 inches or more from the monitor. Try to position yourself at least 40 inches from other monitors as radiation is emitted from the backs and sides.

• To control eye strain, check the brightness and contrast of your surroundings. The brightness should be comfortable to your eyes. Try to keep your monitor close to the hard copy you are keying since that will reduce the amount of refocusing you will have to do when keying large quantities of material.

• Computer work can cause stress. Remind yourself to take ten-minute breaks away from your monitor every hour and look away from the screen occasionally during the rest of the time.

• If you are having eye problems, see your doctor.

Chris: I received this information about reducing possible health problems when using a computer. Please key the information and distribute it to all department managers. They should give the information to each of their office personnel. You will need to prepare a memo to send with the article. Can you do this today? (Thursday)

SKIP

thursday

From the Desk of
Mary Andrews
Human Resources and Development

A
T
C

Chris—   *excel*

Use a spreadsheet to make a Check Register for the week of January 16-20 for the Allied Technology Corporation Special Projects Fund. Use these categories: Check; Date; Payee; Payment; Deposit; Balance. Sort entries by date.

Enter the following information:

From the Desk of
Mary Andrews
Human Resources and Development

A
T
C

Balance on Jan. 16 was 3,887.16

Check No. 600 to First National Bank for $412.22 on Jan. 16; #603 on Jan. 16 for $86.36 to Carol Gild; #604 to Metro Insurance Co. on Jan. 17 for $256.89; #607 on Jan. 19 for $679 to Best Telephone Co.; #608 on Jan. 20 to Justin Marks for $328.78; #602 to City Gas Co. for $75.73 on Jan. 16; #601 on Jan. 16 to Global Electric Co. for $89.98; Deposit on Jan. 17 for $1,056.87; #606 to M. G. Skelly for $403.45 on Jan. 18; #605 for $117.46 to D. R. Fein on Jan. 17

—by Thursday

From the Desk of
Mary Andrews
Human Resources and Development

A
T
C

Thurs.—Key the following information on a Purchase Order Form and send it to the Purchasing Department. Ship via: Fast Freight Company and Purchase Order No. is 8544.

10 boxes Redline paper #34545B @ $12.50 per box
24 packages Springline clips #543A @ 5.75 per box
15 dozen Blue Tip gold pens # 2323D @ $57 per dozen

The company to order these items from is:

DONALLEY SUPPLY COMPANY
4554 ADAMS STREET
OMAHA, NE 68144

Please do this today. Thanks!

Parse quickbooks together

Friday

From the Desk of
Mary Andrews
Human Resources and Development

A
T
C

Here are my expenses from last week's meeting in New York City. Fill out an Employee Expense Voucher for me. Dept. code is 344, Authorization No. is 5655, my Soc. Sec. No. is 402-455-98xx. The purpose of the trip was to present a proposal. Leave the spaces blank on the far right side of the voucher.

Left—Jan. 17, 3:30 p.m.
Returned—Jan. 20, 7:30 p.m.
Hotel—$89 per night plus 12% tax
Meals—Mon., $55, Tues., $87, Wed., $54, Thurs., $45
Taxi—$30 on Mon., $45 Thurs.
Air—$340

I had duplicating fees of $30 on Tuesday, Fax Fees of $29 on Wed., and Supplies of $60 on Thurs.

Do this by Friday since I need to be reimbursed as soon as possible!

make employee voucher

...drews

...d Development

A
T
C

—Pull up the letter from the disk that contains information about my seminar fees (Marysfee.ltr). Send it by Friday to Mr. Jack Swanson, First Bank of Commerce, 3456 Federal Building, Kearney, NE 68847. Use the following figures:

Seminar dates = July 11 and 12, ----

$75 per person, per day—minimum of 20 per day
Meals—$45 per day
400 miles @ .30 per mile
Hotel—$85 per day

skip

Mary Andrews

powerpoint memo attached list of names

Allied Technology Corporation

Human Resources and Development Department Manager
402-555-4445

On Tuesday, February 21, I am making a presentation to the office personnel of Allied Technology Corporation who have joined our company since last January. Many are not following the proper company procedures and need some reinforcing. I need transparency masters for the following items, which you will find in the <u>Company Procedures Manual</u>.

Telephone Etiquette, Time-Wasters, Time Management (1 hour)
Resources (30 min.)
Appointment Scheduling (30 min.)
Filing Guidelines (30 min.)
Finding Lost Records (30 min.)
Salutations Commonly Used (40 min.)

You decide what needs to be on the transparency masters--one to five words for each item listed should be enough (occasionally, you may need to use more words). Attendees will have handouts on the materials so they can follow along and make notes.

Also, make all arrangements for the presentation, which should be held in Conference Room 310. It should run from 8 a.m. until noon with two 10-minute breaks. We need coffee, pop, and muffins available throughout the morning. Prepare a memo for the personnel who will be attending. Key the attached list of names of personnel who have joined us since January 1 of last year. Also, send a memo to the department managers of those who should attend telling them about the seminar. Ask them to make arrangements for their personnel to attend the seminar. On each memo, list the employees who should attend from that department.

Give me the ~~transparency masters,~~ Powerpoint a copy of all the memos, the list of new employees, and a list of all the things you have done to prepare for the presentation plus a schedule of the day's program by Friday.

Friday

Mary Andrews

Allied Technology Corporation

**Human Resources and Development
Department Manager
402-555-4445**

List of Allied Technology Corporation Personnel
Who Have Joined the Company Since Last January 1

Name	Department
Betty Friend	Marketing
Carol Johns	Accounting
Sarah Fleet	Purchasing
Jerry Walters	Purchasing
Lynne Bombara	Accounting
Mary Monte	Purchasing
Steve Ortman	Legal
William Port	Accounting
Larry Wood	Legal
Wendy Engal	Accounting
Abdul Brit	Purchasing
Bev Skalter	Legal
Jack Hubbard	Marketing
Gary Perez	Legal
Jim Murtz	Legal
Sam Dough	Purchasing
Paul Glover	Accounting

w/137

From the Desk of
Mary Andrews
Human Resources and Development

A
T
C

Chris—

I want to contact a business acquaintance in France tomorrow (Friday). When is a good time to call? Remember that it is later in the day there than it is here in Omaha.

Email

(Students: Check the *Company Procedures Manual*. Omaha is in the Central Standard Time zone—CST.)

INTEROFFICE MEMORANDUM

To: Mary Andrews
From: Lee Chung, Legal Department
Date: January 26, ——
Subject: Legal Paragraphs on Disk

Do you have someone who can put these legal paragraphs on disk so that they can be retrieved when necessary? My administrative assistant is ill this week and I will need some of this information by Friday. Thanks!

Chris—Can you do this for Lee by Friday? His administrative assistant will probably not be in next week either, as she has had surgery.

Save each paragraph to your disk and use its identifying number such as P1A, P2A, etc., for the file name. Lee will have the information that will help him to determine which paragraphs he wants to use in his documents.

After you have saved each paragraph to a separate file, print one copy of each. The hard copies will be filed in our office.

Legal Paragraphs Saved to Disk

Paragraph 1A

Enclosed pursuant to Paragraph (f) of Rule 14c-5 issued under the Securities Exchange Act of 1945, are seven copies of the Annual Report to Shareholders for the fiscal year ended December 31, ---- being mailed today by first-class mail to shareholders of the above company.

Paragraph 2A

I am advised by the Corporation's accountants that the financial statements appearing in such annual reports do not reflect a change from the preceding year in any accounting principles or practices or in the method of applying any such principles or practices.

Paragraph 3A

_____ copies of the annual report are also being mailed to the _____ upon which the Corporation's Common Stock is listed.

Paragraph 1B

_____, being duly sworn, says that:

1. I am a member of the firm of _____, attorneys for the defendant in the above entitled action, and I am familiar with all the proceedings heretofore had herein. This affidavit is submitted in support of defendant's motion to change the place of trial in this action from _____ to _____, on the ground of convenience of material witnesses, and the ends of justice will be promoted thereby.

Paragraph 2B

The action was brought to recover damages alleged to have occurred to plaintiff's property while under the control of defendant.

Paragraph 3B

This action was commenced by the service of a summons and complaint on _____, copies of which are annexed hereto as Exhibits "A" and "B." On _____, defendant served its answer, a copy of which is annexed hereto as Exhibit "C."

SKIP

Paragraph 4B

The convenience of material witnesses and the ends of justice will be promoted by the change of the place of trial of this action from _____ to _____, since the defendant, in order to meet and disprove the various allegations in the complaint, will be compelled, upon the trial of this action, to call as witnesses a number of people, all of whom are residents of the City of New York.

Paragraph 5B

The following are the names and residences of necessary witnesses who will be produced and examined by the defendant at the trial:

(1)_____

(2)_____

(3)_____

(4)_____

Paragraph 1C

LAST WILL AND TESTAMENT

I, _____, residing at _____, do hereby declare this to be my Last Will and Testament, hereby revoking any and all other wills and codicils by me at any time heretofore made.

Paragraph 2C

FIRST: I direct that my just debts and funeral and administration expenses be paid as soon after my death as may be practicable.

Paragraph 3C

SECOND: I give and bequeath the sum of _____ ($ _____) to my _____, if he/she survives me. If my _____ should predecease me, then I give and bequeath said sum to his/her issue, in equal shares, per stirpes, or if there be no such issue, then I give and bequeath said sum to _____.

Paragraph 4C

THIRD: All the rest, residue, and remainder of my estate, real and personal and wherever situated, I give, devise, and bequeath to _____, if he/she survives me, or if not to my _____, if he/she survives me. If both of the above predecease me, I give, devise, and bequeath my residuary estate to my _____ in equal shares, per stirpes, or if there be no such issue, to _____.

SKIP

From the Desk of
Mary Andrews
Human Resources and Development

A T C

merge Dept managers

Chris—

Tuesday you keyed an article entitled "Professional Attire Pays Big Dividends in the Office Environment." Send a copy of this article to each of the other four department managers. Attach the copy to a memo from me which reads:

Please emphasize to your department employees the importance of proper attire in our offices. Some of our employees are getting a little lax in this area. We have even had a few calls from customers who have noticed a certain change in professional attitude among some of our employees. We must point out that our reason for being here is to please the customers.

Please send this out today.—M A

A T C

...ndrews
...nd Development

Chris—

Some of the newer employees are having difficulty with the telephone system. Find information for me on the following: Auto redial, Call forwarding, Caller ID, Camp on, Call return, Call waiting, Conferencing, Memory, and Speakerphone.

Prepare a memo for office personnel and attach a copy of your research.

I need this by 3 p.m. today.

M A

Attachment to email

From the Desk of
Mary Andrews
Human Resources and Development

A
T
C

Chris—

We need to add a section to our <u>Company Procedures Manual</u> on different kinds of mail processing such as first-class mail, priority mail, second-class mail, third-class mail, fourth-class mail, express mail, special delivery, registered mail, insured mail, certified mail, and COD mail. Can you research this for me and prepare the material in an appropriate format so it can be added to the <u>Company Procedures Manual</u>? (Check the manual to see how some of the other information has been formatted.)

This should be helpful to all company personnel, not just the new employees. I would like to see it by Friday noon.

M A

---

add to research on phone definitions of terms

us postal

Friday Assignment (January 27)

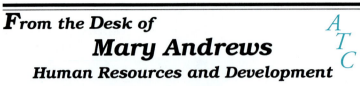

I will be leaving on Feb. 22 (returning Feb. 25) for Minneapolis for a conference. I need to be at my first meeting by 3:30 p.m. Wednesday and want to be back home by 7:00 p.m. on Saturday. Air fare will be $280; hotel will be $85 plus 8.5% tax per night for three nights.

Check on the price of a rental car for me. I want a medium-sized car and will need it from Wednesday p.m. until Saturday p.m. (The usual rate is about $50 per day plus $.50 per mile. I will probably drive about 200 miles.) Meals will be about $60 per day. Other expenses will total about $70.

Fill out a Travel Authorization form. I need to sign it before I leave today (Friday). The Purchasing Department will add the Travel Authorization number later. Have the ticket charged to the company credit card. Return copy of approved authorization to me.

M

(Students: When figuring car rental rates on the Travel Authorization form, use $50 per day plus $.50 per mile.)

Mary Andrews

Allied
Technology
Corporation

Human Resources and Development
Department Manager
402-555-4445

Key these items on purchase order forms—calculate extensions and totals. Add 6% sales tax. All items are shipped via Fast Freight Company—Need today (Friday). Prepare a fax sheet for each so we can speed up the process. See Company Procedures Manual for fax form. Use all caps on addresses.

Purchase Order to Mike Stettson, Main Street Wholesalers, 4589 Arnold Avenue, Omaha, NE 68124 (Fax No. 402-555-9878)

Purchase Order Number: 6509867
Terms: 2/10, n/30

Items Ordered: 40 dozen R-1 chocolate chip cookies @ $2.95 per dozen; 25 cases of H-2 welcome napkins @ $55 per case; 20 boxes of W-5 blue plastic forks @ $12 per box

———————————

Purchase Order to Martin Manufacturing Company, 2312 13th Street, Omaha, NE 68102 (Fax No. 402-555-2333)

Purchase Order Number: 453332
Terms: 2/10, n/30

Items Ordered: a dozen Springbrock brown chairs, No. T9076 @ $325 each

———————————

Purchase Order to Daniel's Quality Products, 3256 Montrose Avenue, Omaha, NE 68144 (Fax No. 402-555-7766)

Purchase Order Number: R23541
Terms: 2/10, n/30

Items Ordered: 3 W334 Sonet tape recorders @ $145.98 each; 2 boxes X324 Benson tapes, size 1 inch @ $15.99 per box

quick books

From the Desk of
Mary Andrews
Human Resources and Development

A T C

Prepare a list of the Canadian provinces and their abbreviations—today (Friday).

SKIP

From the Desk of
Mary Andrews
Human Resources and Development

A T C

Prepare a Certificate of Attendance similar to the sample in the <u>Company Procedures Manual</u>. Leave a place to fill in the name of the workshop and date. We'll use it as a master for each of the workshops we are conducting in the next few months.

—Can you do this today?

Seminar attendance merge

From the Desk of
Mary Andrews
Human Resources and Development

A T C

Retrieve the list of seminar attendees that you keyed in Wed. from the computer (sematend.lst), and make a set of labels. Also, complete the information on a Certificate of Attendance for each attendee. I will be doing the seminar on Tuesday, February 7, ----, in Kearney, NE. The name of the seminar is "Dealing With Current Office Trends." Can you do this today?

From the Desk of
Mary Andrews
Human Resources and Development

A T C

We need two sets of labels for all of the companies on Customer List No. 56—today (Friday). You keyed the names into the database on Monday.

Skip

From the Desk of
Mary Andrews
Human Resources and Development

Write a letter to each of the February 7 seminar participants and thank them for attending. Include the certificates you prepared. (Today— Friday) We will use the labels you have prepared and will send these out in 9 x 12 manila envelopes after the seminar.

Laptop

letter
merge

Mary Andrews

*Allied
Technology
Corporation*

**Human Resources and Development
Department Manager
402-555-4445**

Chris:

Use Outlook to Calendar

Make a list of all the activities that I will be involved in February through December and let me see it today (Friday). You can enter the information into my calendar next week after I have approved it. This will include all workshops from the flyer you keyed on Monday (4M-F). Make a note showing dates when I have more than one thing scheduled. I will need to make arrangements for someone else to supervise the arrangements on these days.

Here are some additional activities in which I will be involved:

February 7	8-5 seminar in Kearney, NE
February 8	3-5 Interview candidate for opening
February 9	9-12 Interview more candidates
February 28	All-day meeting (9-5) at Brown, Inc.
March 22-25	Seminar presentation in Oxnard, CA
April 17-21	Convention in Boston
April 26	Department Retreat at Park View (all day)
May 15-16	Seminar presentation in Chicago
May 17	Managers' In-House Retreat—all day
June 13	Seminar here—9-5—for Electronics, Inc.
June 23	Business Women of America—presentation at noon. Block out morning and p.m. until 3:30
June 30	Luncheon for visiting branch managers—block out entire day in case of any special meetings that may be called
July 11-12	Workshop in Kearney, NE

From the Desk of
Mary Andrews
Human Resources and Development

A T C

I received this from one of our new administrative assistants. It needs some corrections. Will you work on it today (Friday)? Add proofreading symbols and explain to her on Monday what you did and why. She can rekey it on Monday.

SKIP

a problem

view sexual

the first, an

sexual

e work

970s, and

employe

recognis

VII.

(EECC)

e sexual

condut of a

that sever

rights

scrimination

n the the

- • Unsolicited and unwelcmoe flirtations, advances or propositons
- • Displa of sexualy suggestvie objects or pitures
- • Leerign
- • Physicle or sexual asault
- • Whistlin, catcalls
- • Abuse of familiaritiesor diminutives such as "honey", 'baby', "dear"
- • Sexual or intrusive questions about imploye's personal life
- • Dirty jokes offensive gestures
- • Explicit descriptions ofthe harasser's onw sexual experiences
- • Unnecessary, unwanted physical contact such as touching, hugging pinching,   patting, kissing

What Is Sexual Harrassment?

Although sexual harrassment has long been recognized as a problem in the workplace, it is relatively new as a legal issue.

The enactment of of Title VII of the 1964 civil rights act view sexual harrassment as a kindof employment discrimniation.

The la recognises 2 categories of sexual harrassment. In the first, an empoyer or supervisor makes sexual advancesand links terms of ofemployment to the workers response. In the second category, sexual advances are sever and pervasiv enough that the create a hostile work enviromnent for the employe.

Courts first began to consider sexual harrassment in the 1970s,and specialists point to a 1976 case bought by a Justice Department employe against an employer as a breakthrough that led other courts to recognis harrassment "based on sex" to be within the meaning of Title VII.

In 1980 the Equal Employment Opportunity Commission (EECC) issued guidelines that defined sexual harrassment as "unwelcome sexual advances, requestsfor sexual favors, and other verbal orphysical condut of a sexual nature' in the workplace.

In 1986 the Supreme Court ruled in a unaninous desision that sever or pervasive sexual harrassment of an employe by a supervisor violatedfederal law. The case was hailed at the time as a civil rights landmarck.

The courts began calling sexual harrassment a from of discrimination because it so clearly hampered the ability women to funckon in the the workplace.

Sexual Harrassment: Examples

* Unsolicited and unwelcmoe flirtations, advances or propositons
* Displa of sexualy suggestvie objects or pitures
* Leerign
* Physicle or sexual asault
* Whistlin, catcalls
* Abuse of familiaritiesor diminutives such as "honey", "baby', "dear"
* Sexual or intrusive questions about imploye's personal life
* Dirty jokes offensive gestures
* Explicit descriptions ofthe harasser's onw sexual experiences
* Unnecessary, unwanted physical contact such as touching, hugging pinching, patting, kissing

Sexual Harrassment: If It Happens to You

Sexual harrassment includes any attention that focuses on a workers sex rather than her status as an employe. If this happen, do the following:

• Tell harasser the behavior is unwelcome and it should stop; ignoring it will usually not discourage the harasser

• If situation persists, report it to supervisor or that of harasser

• Keep a writen record of what harasser says and does, whom saw it how you responded, to who you reported it.

• Discus situation with co-workers who have experience similar harrassment

• If your company has a greivance procedure, or if you are are a union member, file a foraml complaint

• If these steps fial, file a complain with the Equal Employment Opportunity Commission or file a claim with private attorney

$$\begin{matrix}A\\T\\C\end{matrix}$$

INTEROFFICE MEMORANDUM

To: Mary Andrews
From: Sally
Date: January 15, ----
Subject: Inventoried Items Requested

H-444, Room 40, CD-ROM, 1995, Repairs: 2-6-95
G-45, Room 43, Calculator, 1994, Repairs: 4-5-95, 5-9-95
F-2356, Monitor, Room 45, 1994, Repairs: 3-25-94,
5-23-94, 7-3-94
H-14, Room 45, Computer, 1996, Repairs: None
F-890, Room 42, Modem, 1996, Repairs: None
G-22, Monitor, Room 42, 1995, Repairs: None
F-3121, Room 47, Printer, 1995, Repairs: 3-7-95

This information was gathered by Sally. Enter it on an Inventory Worksheet Form—

Prepare a report about your recommendations as to whether equipment needs to be kept longer or replaced.

—need Friday by 10 a.m.

Mary Andrews

Allied
Technology
Corporation

Human Resources and Development
Department Manager
402-555-4445

We need a registration form to be used for the meeting and luncheon on Thursday, March 30. The meeting will be from 10 a.m. until 4 p.m. in Columbus Hall, 4567 Main Street, here in town. Lunch will be served from 11:45 a.m. until 1:00 p.m.

The menu will be ham salad, buttered peas, fresh fruit, rolls, coffee/tea/milk, and cherry ice cream. The price is $12.95, which includes gratuity. We need a response by Monday, March 27. Be sure to ask how many reservations will be needed from each company—we also need the names of those who will be attending the luncheon. We can bill the companies of those attending.

The meeting is for the "Technology is for Everyone" seminar. Columbus Hall will hold 500 people. We may have almost that many attend.

—Let me see the form you prepare by noon today.

Mary

Mary
Phone after hours
Call 503-399-6094

From the Desk of
Mary Andrews
Human Resources and Development

A
T
C

You did such a nice job on the new page on mailing procedures for the <u>Company Procedures Manual</u> *that I would like you now to add information on filing materials. Find information about the following and then prepare pages for the* <u>Company Procedures Manual</u> *following the format of other items in the manual. Title the information "Filing Procedures" and prepare paragraphs about inspecting, indexing, coding, cross referencing, sorting, and storing. Also include information on filing supplies such as guides, file folders, labels, out cards, and out folders.*

A
T
C

...drews
...and Development

I would like to see what you have put together for this project by 4 p.m. today (Friday). There are several office reference manuals in the front office that should be helpful in finding this information.

Mary

skip

From the Desk of
Mary Andrews
Human Resources and Development

A
T
C

Excel *Laptop*

Prepare a pie chart with the following information. Make it large enough so that it can be used as a master for an overhead transparency. I will be needing it for a talk I am giving early next week. Put it on my desk before you leave this evening. (Friday)

How Communication Time Is Spent

Listening	45%
Writing	9%
Reading	16%
Speaking	30%

From the Desk of
Mary Andrews
Human Resources and Development

A
T
C

The cassette I put on your desk has an article entitled "What You Need to Know About Health Insurance." Transcribe it and send a copy to each of the department managers. Prepare a memo from me indicating that this information should be shared with their employees. In the section "Insurance Terminology," the sentence describing "Coverage" should read, "An insurance policy must indicate the extent of the health benefits, and will usually spell out exclusions as well." Please change.

Skip

by 3 p.m. today

From the Desk of
Mary Andrews
Human Resources and Development

A
T
C

Chris

Transcribe the article entitled "Better Working Conditions Means More Productivity." After the fifth point, the first sentence should read, "A good ergonomically designed chair is adjustable." The tape is on my desk. Make two copies. I will need the copies before I leave this evening (Friday).

ACTIVITY TIME CHART

DAY	ASSIGNMENT	TIME	ACTIVITY	WHEN COMPLETED/ COMMENTS	
				Due Day	Time
Monday January 23					

ACTIVITY TIME CHART

DAY	ASSIGNMENT	TIME	ACTIVITY	WHEN COMPLETED/ COMMENTS	
				Due Day	Time
Tuesday January 24					

ACTIVITY TIME CHART

DAY	ASSIGNMENT	TIME	ACTIVITY	WHEN COMPLETED/ COMMENTS	
				Due Day	Time
Wednesday January 25					

ACTIVITY TIME CHART

DAY	ASSIGNMENT	TIME	ACTIVITY	WHEN COMPLETED/ COMMENTS	
				Due Day	Time
Thursday January 26					

ACTIVITY TIME CHART

DAY	ASSIGNMENT	TIME	ACTIVITY	WHEN COMPLETED/ COMMENTS	
				Due Day	Time
Friday January 27					

EMPLOYEE EVALUATION

Rating Scale*

Quantity	O	E	G	F	NI
Efficient use of time and resources	❏	❏	❏	❏	❏
Speed of completion of tasks and procedures	❏	❏	❏	❏	❏

Quality	O	E	G	F	NI
Accuracy of work	❏	❏	❏	❏	❏
Ability to make decisions	❏	❏	❏	❏	❏

Work Habits	O	E	G	F	NI
Responsibility	❏	❏	❏	❏	❏
Creative drive	❏	❏	❏	❏	❏
Dependability	❏	❏	❏	❏	❏
Punctuality	❏	❏	❏	❏	❏
Open-mindedness	❏	❏	❏	❏	❏

Personal Relations	O	E	G	F	NI
Appearance	❏	❏	❏	❏	❏
Cooperativeness	❏	❏	❏	❏	❏

Adaptability	O	E	G	F	NI
Alertness	❏	❏	❏	❏	❏
Flexibility	❏	❏	❏	❏	❏
Innovativeness	❏	❏	❏	❏	❏

Supervision	O	E	G	F	NI
Delegation of responsibility	❏	❏	❏	❏	❏
Fairness	❏	❏	❏	❏	❏

General	O	E	G	F	NI
Ambition	❏	❏	❏	❏	❏
Enthusiasm	❏	❏	❏	❏	❏
Honesty	❏	❏	❏	❏	❏
Loyalty	❏	❏	❏	❏	❏

*O = Outstanding   F = Fair
E = Excellent   NI = Needs improvement
G = Good

FAX COVER SHEET

DATE:

TO:

FAX NUMBER:

FROM:

**NUMBER OF PAGES
INCLUDING THIS
COVER SHEET:**

MESSAGE:

**If any part of this fax
transmission is missing
or not clearly received,
please call:**

NAME:

PHONE NUMBER:

A
T
C

INTEROFFICE MEMORANDUM

To:
From:
Date:
Subject:

Series Title:				Form ID Number:

Inventory Worksheet

Year	Number	Location	Equipment	Repair Record

Department:	Store's Signature:	Date:

Series Title:				Form ID Number:

Inventory Worksheet

Year	Number	Location	Equipment	Repair Record

Department:	Store's Signature:	Date:

Allied
Technology
Corporation

2323 North Hamilton Avenue • Omaha, NE 68144-0111
(402) 555-5555 • Fax (402) 555-5444 • E-mail hfm@aolemc.com

From the Desk of Chris Downing

Allied
Technology
Corporation

Human Resources and Development Department
402-555-3352

*A*llied *T*echnology *C*orporation

2323 North Hamilton Avenue • Omaha, NE 68144-0111
(402) 555-5555 • Fax (402) 555-5444 • E-mail hfm@aolemc.com

Purchase Order

To:

Purchase Order No.:
Date:
Terms:
Shipped Via:

Quantity	Description	Price	Per	Total

VACATION REQUEST

EMPLOYEE

NAME		DATE	
EMPLOYEE I.D.		DEPARTMENT	
EMPLOYMENT STARTING DATE		TIME EMPLOYED	
VACATION DAYS AVAILABLE		AS OF	

PREFERRED REQUEST			SECONDARY REQUEST		
START	END	APPROVAL	START	END	APPROVAL

Employee Signature _____ Submit Date _____

FORM TO BE SUBMITTED TO DIRECT SUPERVISOR FOR REVIEW

DAYS APPROVED		DAYS REMAINING	

Comments: _____

_____

_____

Supervisor's Signature _____ Date _____

Have a Great Break!

VACATION REQUEST

EMPLOYEE

NAME		DATE	
EMPLOYEE I.D.		DEPARTMENT	
EMPLOYMENT STARTING DATE		TIME EMPLOYED	
VACATION DAYS AVAILABLE		AS OF	

PREFERRED REQUEST			SECONDARY REQUEST		
START	END	APPROVAL	START	END	APPROVAL

Employee Signature _____ Submit Date _____

FORM TO BE SUBMITTED TO DIRECT SUPERVISOR FOR REVIEW

DAYS APPROVED		DAYS REMAINING	

Comments: _____

_____

_____

Supervisor's Signature _____ Date _____

Have a Great Break!

Allied Technology Corporation
VOUCHER OF EMPLOYEE EXPENSE
Reimbursement for Travel only

Department Name or Code:	Invoice Number:
Authorization Number:	If Other than Co. Car was used, Enter License Plate #:
Telephone Number:	Owner Name:
Social Security Number:	Request Number:
	Purpose of Trip:

Employee Name

Dept. Branch Address

City, State _____ Zip

LIST EXPENSES BY DAY. ATTACH ALL RECEIPTS FOR EXPENSES EXCLUDING ITEMS UNDER $5.00. ITEMIZE ALL MISCELLANEOUS EXPENSES AND ENTER ALL DEPARTURE AND ARRIVAL TIMES.

DATE	LOCAL TIME	PLACE CITY AND STATE	MEALS $ AMT.	LODGING $ AMT.	MOTOR VEHICLE MILES	$ AMT.	MISCELLANEOUS DESCRIPTION	$ AMT.	TAXI ETC. $ AMT.	TOTAL $ AMT.
	DEP.									
	ARR.									
	DEP.									
	ARR.									
	DEP.									
	ARR.									
	DEP.									
	ARR.									
	DEP.									
	ARR.									
	DEP.									
	ARR.									
	DEP.									
	ARR.									
TOTALS →			$	$		$		$	$	$

I request reimbursement from Allied Technology Corporation for the above expenses incurred by myself in the line and operations of duty and declare that the above statement of charges is a true and accurate account of expenses for which payment has not been made heretofore by Allied Technology Corporation.

APPROVED

SIGNATURE OF CLAIMANT _____ DATE _____ REQUIRED SIGNATURE OF SUPERVISOR, REGIONAL

Quizzes

Capitalization Quiz

Directions: Some of the following sentences contain capitalization errors. Using proof-reading marks, indicate what changes need to be made.

1. Did you know that dr. singer's office is in the medical arts building?

2. We will visit the caribbean on the famous love boat.

3. All of our apple computers are being purchased at a discount price.

4. The fair will be held in lincoln, nebraska.

5. When will governor smith arrive?

6. Will professor smartz come to the meeting?

7. Who is the secretary who will take the notes at the meeting?

8. Today mayor-elect maria romero will take office.

9. The company will honor its retiring officers.

10. Your subscription to <u>music world</u> will expire next month.

11. We must purchase the book entitled <u>history of the americas</u> for our class.

12. Did you see the article entitled "spring is just a month away" in the journal?

13. The board of governors will meet at noon.

14. We hope that president adams will not be left out of the festivities.

15. We will meet with professor brown over the noon hour.

16. They live on the west side of the city.

17. Please send this information to billie brown, chair of the budget committee.

18. We will be traveling east when we get to that city.

19. Most county offices close at 4:30 p.m.

20. Henry jones, secretary of labor, will be our speaker.

Envelope Quiz

Directions: Complete the following sentences by writing the correct answer(s) on the lines provided.

1. The letters OCR mean _____.

2. When placing "PLEASE FORWARD" on an envelope, it should be placed

    _____.

3. Use a _____ typeface when addressing an envelope.

4. To expedite handling of returned mail, it is appropriate to _____.

5. The last line of the envelope address should contain _____.

6. An envelope that is 9 1/2 inches by 4 1/8 inches is called a _____.

7. When sending a two-page letter or a one-page letter with an enclosure, use a

    _____.

8. The proper format for keying the name and address of the recipient is to use

    _____ spacing and _____ format.

9. When keying the state in the recipient's address, use a _____.

10. The recipient's address should be placed at the _____.

Filing Quiz

Directions: At the left of the items in Part A, place the appropriate letter from Part B that makes the item true. Some letters in Part B will not be used.

Part A

___ 1. If you spend a great deal of time trying to find items in the files

___ 2. It is time to add another folder when

___ 3. Keep a record of who has checked out a file so

___ 4. In order to be sure that files have been correctly replaced

___ 5. For the most uniform results in filing

___ 6. An in-basket on your desk should be used for

___ 7. An "out" sheet is used

___ 8. When maintaining a subject file

___ 9. To keep files up-to-date, it is important to

___ 10. Each file drawer should have

___ 11. A file cabinet may tip over if

___ 12. It is a good idea to file at

___ 13. Transfer

___ 14. Documents should be placed

___ 15. The heading of a document

Part B

a. you can follow up on it if it is not returned within a reasonable amount of time
b. develop a filing manual and insist on its use
c. throw files away after six months
d. replace the files yourself
e. place in alphabetical order
f. a file folder is three-fourths of an inch full
g. returned files
h. you leave two upper drawers open at once
i. to help you to know what was taken, when, and by whom
j. file every day
k. keep an index of file captions so that duplication will not occur
l. the same time every day and at a time when interruptions are few
m. replace broken guides
n. old files to a permanent storage area
o. with the latest date at the front of the folder—in chronological order
p. should be at the left of the folder
q. replace broken guides
r. three to four inches of working space
s. you may need to add more guides

Job Description for Administrative Assistant Quiz

Directions: The *Company Procedures Manual* contains a list of activities that the administrative assistant should be able to perform. List ten of those activities; write a paragraph for *each* activity indicating why you can satisfactorily perform that activity in the office in which you plan to work.

Letter Parts Quiz

Directions: Below is an example of a letter that is being sent out by Allied Technology Corporation. Place the name of the letter parts on the lines below.

Allied
Technology
Corporation

2323 North Hamilton Avenue • Omaha, NE 68144-0111
1   (402) 555-5555 • Fax (402) 555-5444 • E-mail hfm@aolemc.com

2 January 24, ——

3 Mr. Mi Chung
   Burwell Supply Company
   6556 Winter Street
   Burwell, FL 33105-6543

4 Dear Mr. Chung

5 Your order was received last Friday. Your products have always been some of the best sellers in our stores. However, there has been a problem with this order.

We have had several customers return the contact paper (Item No. 3454) because they say it does not stick well. We tried several of the rolls on our own shelves and found that the customers' complaints were valid. Our order for this product was quite large; I have enclosed the paperwork.

Please let us know what can be done about this shipment. Our customers are eager for a replacement.

6 Sincerely

7 ALLIED TECHNOLOGY CORPORATION

8 John Perry, Manager

9 spc

10 Enclosure

11 c Sumi Qui
      William Seily

1. _____   7. _____

2. _____   8. _____

3. _____   9. _____

4. _____   10. _____

5. _____   11. _____

6. _____

Numbers Quiz

Directions: Some of the following sentences contain number usage errors. Circle the errors and write the corrected sentence in the space below.

1. The directory shows that 7th Avenue begins at Apple Street.

2. 345 new subscriptions were received as a result of our survey.

3. Your subscription expires in 6 months.

4. The cost is 39 cents each.

5. Nearly 3/4 of our clients are men.

6. This note will be due in thirty days.

7. The exact due date is October 30th.

8. Company headquarters is located at 2,876 Elmwood Drive.

9. Besides managing her $40,000,000-year company, Ms. Smith finds time for civic activities.

10. This money will purchase 400 6-foot boards.

11. You owe me $30.00 for the dress.

12. The shipment arrived with five chairs, 16 tables, and 23 desks.

13. 2,000,000 people came to the demonstration.

14. Interest on those bonds increased three percent last year.

15. A package of six sells for 50 cents.

16. One of her 3 suggestions was to buy the property.

17. There are 100s of excuses for not going.

18. Your order was shipped on June 6th.

19. By 1990 15 people will have been in that position.

20. She ordered six pencils, five pens, and sixteen pads.

21. We will be there at ten o'clock.

22. He will soon be 30.

23. There were approximately 55 people at the picnic.

24. The bank account number is thirty-three.

25. We live at 3556 North 8th Avenue.

26. Their fifth child was named Greg.

27. There are 55 people at the party.

28. Look on page 6 of the manual.

29. We live at Three Marble Boulevard.

30. 645 books were given away by the library.

Parliamentary Terms Quiz

Directions: Match Column A with the definitions in Column B by placing the correct letter of the description in Column B next to the matching item in Column A.

Column A

_____ 1. Amend

_____ 2. Teller

_____ 3. Nomination

_____ 4. Main motion

_____ 5. Out of order

_____ 6. Precedence

_____ 7. Convene

_____ 8. Ballot

_____ 9. Adopt

_____ 10. Second

_____ 11. Order of business

_____ 12. Standing committee

_____ 13. Preamble

_____ 14. Carried

_____ 15. Majority vote

Column B

a. number of members who must be present to conduct business legally

b. to cancel a motion or report so it will not be considered at any time

c. approval of a proposed motion for consideration by the group

d. a rule of an organization

e. to open a meeting formally

f. more than half the number legally voting

g. discussion on a matter before the group

h. a list of official business to be covered at a meeting

i. an introduction to a constitution or resolution stating its purpose

j. a paper or mechanical device used to record votes privately

k. not in keeping with accepted parliamentary procedure at a particular time

l. member who assists in conducting voting by ballot

m. to approve

n. the sequence of items of business to be consisdered at the meeting

o. order of priority or rank

p. approved by the required number of votes

q. committee set up to handle all business related to a certain subject

r. a motion presented to a group for consideration

s. to change

t. a formal proposal of a person for an office

Proofreading Quiz

Directions: Column A is correct. Using proofreading marks, correct Columns B and C.

Column A	Column B	Column C
Richard Freidworth	Richard Freidworht	Rickhard Freidworth
346-896-9887	345-686-9887	345-896-9888
Mrs. Betty Hopewell	Ms. Betty Hopwell	Miss Bettie Hopewell
5655 Orange Boulevard	5655 Oange Boulvard	5565 Orang Boulevarde
Trenton, NJ 98848-0515	Trenton, NY 9884-0515	Trenton, NY
Dr. Ivan Ricks	Mr. Ivan Richs	Mr. Ivan Riches
34 Northeast Drive	355 NorthEast Drive	34 North East Drive
Houston, TX 77001	Houston, Texas 77 001	Houston, Texes 78001
$436,365,298.90	$446,365,289.90	$436,366,298.09
508-50-9099	508-40-9009	506-60-9099
#678,567,234,440	#678,567,243,440	#678,576,432,044
Sigfried Clapper	Sigfried Clapper	Sigfried Clapper
6677 Chester Avenue	6677 Chester Avanue	6677 Chester Avenue
Omaha, NE 68108	Omaha, NE	Omah, NB 68108
456	456	456
2354	2545	2354
132,333,555	133,333,555	132,334,555
13-6789-9876	12-6789 9876	12-6789-9876
45	45	45
45	45	54
29	29	29-
29	92	29

Punctuation Quiz

Part A

Directions: Insert the correct punctuation in the following sentences. Indicate the proper punctuation category by filling in the blank at the left of the sentence with one of the following (some sentences have more than one answer):

1.	Parenthetical Comments	7.	Independent Clause—Semicolon
2.	Apposition	8.	Independent Clause—No Conjunction
3.	Series	9.	And Omitted
4.	Dependent Clause	10.	Omission Commas
5.	Introductory Words	11.	Illustrative Material
6.	Independent Clause	12.	Colon

_____ 1. Please bring cake cookies ice cream and nuts to the party.

_____ 2. As a point of reference turn to page 6.

_____ 3. We will have many good times in the future and we will be friends forever.

_____ 4. We have offices in Omaha Des Moines and Denver.

_____ 5. We will be able to go also.

_____ 6. Our supply order must be submitted by April 30 consequently please send it soon.

_____ 7. She is a sweet adorable child.

_____ 8. Betty will come on Thursday too if she can.

_____ 9. We will hire the following Bill Brown Henry Jones and Bob Baker.

_____ 10. For the duration of the period we will be taking over that department.

_____ 11. Because it was not necessary we did not process the order.

_____ 12. Mary did the washing Ruth did the ironing and I put everything away.

_____ 13. Colorado Travel is located in Denver Colorado

_____ 14. Last week we sold six cars this week just three.

_____ 15. Although short this report contains all the necessary information.

_____ 16. Order these items bread milk cheese butter and cream.

_____ 17. We expect our manager Miss Smith to come to the meeting.

_____ 18. He has interesting thought-provoking ideas.

_____ 19. Our office will be open we will try to process the papers.

_____ 20. Be sure to spell out the states namely Illinois Texas and Maine.

Part B

Directions: Below each of the following sentences, rewrite the sentence using the correct punctuation.

1. Jerry said let the music begin

2. Mary responded the sheet music for the flutes is not here but the band began to play

3. We are all guilty of spouting off sometimes

4. They were shocked at his actions and called him a cheater

5. Betty asked will we be able to afford to go to the movie

6. Brent replied of course we will

7. Sally responded isn't the name of the movie silent spring

8. Honesty the principal said is always the best policy

9. Why did Jill say we will all be late to class

10. Will we be able to have pop and chips at the dance Barry asked

11. Emilio whispered I need to borrow the article entitled the internet is exciting

12. The teacher gave these directions read the chapter carefully and then answer questions 5 through 25 on page 16. Hand in your paper at the beginning of class on Tuesday and be ready for the test on Wednesday

Records Management Quiz

Part A

Directions: Under Column B, indicate the order in which the items in Column A will be filed. An example is provided.

Column A

Betty A. Holtz
Betty C. Holts
Betty B. Holts

Column B

Holts, Betty B.
Holts, Betty C.
Holtz, Betty A.

1. Jack D. Donaldson
    Mary B. Donaldson
    Jerry M. Donaldson

    _____
    _____
    _____

2. Billie Hawks-Jackson
    John Brahms
    Terry Smithford
    Lillie Smith-Bronson

    _____
    _____
    _____
    _____

3. Bernie Van Horn
    Herman Johnson
    Virgil Van Phelps
    Marcy Ackers
    Kathy Smith-Beck
    Jack La Lane
    Betty Des Right

    _____
    _____
    _____
    _____
    _____
    _____
    _____

4. Queen Elizabeth
    Queen Virginia
    King Charles
    Princess Margaret
    Sister Margaret
    Bernice Strenge
    Jack Van Voorhis
    Tracy Smith-Ford
    Tami C. Loomis
    Sister Amelia
    Father Francis
    James C. D. Jackson

    _____
    _____
    _____
    _____
    _____
    _____
    _____
    _____
    _____
    _____
    _____
    _____

5. Dr. Bruce Jackson
    Mr. Bill Bracket
    Captain Jeremy Jerome
    Dr. C. F. Flyn
    Dr. C. F. Flynn
    Captain Jack Sprat
    Captain J. S. Sprat
    Dr. Bruce Billinstown
    Dr. Lisa Winkley
    Mrs. Lisa Winkley

    _____
    _____
    _____
    _____
    _____
    _____
    _____
    _____
    _____
    _____

Column A	**Column B**
6. AAA Club	_____
XYZ Company	_____
Perry Lumber Company	_____
A. C. Holmes and Company	_____
Jackson Supply Company	_____
TYC Electronics	_____
John Meyers Control Company	_____
7. Des Moines Catalog	_____
St. Lawrence River	_____
St. Francis Bookstore	_____
Mt. Rainy Island	_____
St. Louis Clothing Outlet	_____
8. Southwestern Canadian Route	_____
South Western Canada	_____
Western Garden Club	_____
North Western College	_____
Northwestern Mountain Trail	_____
Southeastern Farm Implements	_____
South East Construction Company	_____
Southwestern Charm School	_____
South West Fruit Outlet	_____
9. 5 Star Photos	_____
711 Harlan Office Building	_____
Five Hundred Club	_____
9th Avenue Bank	_____
10. Los Angeles News	_____
Des Moines Register	_____
Lincoln Star	_____
Oklahoma Gazette	_____
Texas Star Reporter	_____
Times News	_____
Changing Times	_____
11. Nebraska Department of Education	_____
California Department of Labor	_____
Oregon Department of Motor Vehicles	_____
12. Mary Bronks	_____
Sister Mary	_____
Father Morgan	_____
3 Star Theater	_____
Dr. Jack Jackson	_____
Dr. Jack C. Jackson	_____
Dr. Jack C. Jacksen	_____
Kansas City Star	_____
St. Charles Chronicle	_____
Pastor Robert Rook	_____

Part B

Directions: At the top of the page is a list of items that must be filed in the proper order. At the bottom of the page, show the proper order of the indexing units and the correct order that they should be placed into the file.

1. Betty Burmer-Stone
2. Jerry S. Connet
3. American Management Association
4. Amos Cook
5. Sammy Su Chung
6. Genior L. S. Americo
7. Mrs. Mary B. L. Springbrook
8. Russell Stover Candies
9. XYZ Car Cleaners
10. Los Angeles Shipping Company
11. Buttons 'n' Bows
12. North West Cattle Company
13. A. C. Cook
14. Northwest Cattle Company
15. Cleveland Gazette
16. Tenth Street Steak House
17. City Post Office
18. Nebraska Department of Revenue
19. 21 Broadway Market
20. Southern Baptist Organization

Key Unit	**Unit 2**	**Unit 3**	**Unit 4**

Redundancy Quiz

Directions: Some employers and employees have a tendency to use extra words and archaic expressions. Indicate under Column B how you would shorten the words or expressions in Column A.

Column A	**Column B**
1. as soon as possible	_____
2. it will be greatly appreciated	_____
3. I would like to thank you	_____
4. for the month of September	_____
5. the majority of our stockholders	_____
6. for your information, the manuscript arrived	_____
7. at this time	_____
8. in view of the fact that	_____
9. in accordance with your request, a refund	_____
10. a large number of people attended	_____
11. the shipment will go forward	_____
12. in due course	_____
13. for the purpose of	_____
14. prior to	_____
15. in the event that	_____
16. give consideration to	_____
17. with regard to	_____
18. it is our understanding that	_____
19. in the near future	_____
20. enclosed please find	_____
21. attached hereto	_____
22. we regret that we will be unable	_____
23. the purpose of this letter is	_____
24. make an adjustment in	_____

Resource Quiz

Directions: Below is a list of resource categories that can be helpful in an office. Under each category, place the name of one specific resource that fits into the category.

1. Almanac

2. Atlas

3. Biography for business

4. Book index

5. Financial report

6. General periodical index

7. Informational service

8. Newspaper and/or periodical

9. U.S. Government sources

10. Name four *sources* of information.

Salutation Quiz

Directions: Indicate under Column B what salutation you would use for the individual(s) listed under Column A. (There may be more than one answer—list as many answers as you think apply.)

Column A   **Column B**

1. To a married couple with the last name of Gray   _____

2. To the stockholders of the company   _____
                                                       _____
                                                       _____
                                                       _____

3. Pat Black   _____
                                                       _____

4. Three single women: Carmen Reyes,   _____
   Betty Brown, Barbara Holt   _____
                                                       _____
                                                       _____

5. To the three women above who are married   _____
                                                       _____
                                                       _____

6. To an organization composed of all men   _____

7. To Shirley Brit, whose courtesy title is unknown   _____
                                                       _____

8. To one man, whose gender is known but not
   his name   _____

9. To Bill Brown, Jim Jones, and Mario Ciummo   _____
                                                       _____
                                                       _____

10. To an organization composed of all women   _____

11. To Jim Black, Peter Chung, and Jane Stewart   _____
                                                       _____

12. To a married couple named Betty Bets and Jack
    Jetters   _____
                                                       _____
                                                       _____

Second-Page Headings and Letter Punctuation Style Quiz

Part A

Directions: There are two approved methods for beginning the second page of a letter. Show how each should be done.

Method No. 1

Method No. 2

Part B

Directions: Two main punctuation styles are used in the salutation and closing of letters. Name them and show how each should be keyed.

Style No. 1

Style No. 2

State Abbreviation Quiz

Directions: Place the correct two-letter abbreviation next to the state name.

_____ 1. Missouri

_____ 2. Utah

_____ 3. Minnesota

_____ 4. Illinois

_____ 5. Hawaii

_____ 6. Wyoming

_____ 7. South Dakota

_____ 8. Pennsylvania

_____ 9. Nebraska

_____ 10. Idaho

_____ 11. Delaware

_____ 12. Iowa

_____ 13. Tennessee

_____ 14. Wisconsin

_____ 15. Ohio

_____ 16. Connecticut

_____ 17. Georgia

_____ 18. Kansas

_____ 19. Mississippi

_____ 20. Washington

_____ 21. West Virginia

_____ 22. Maine

_____ 23. Alabama

_____ 24. Arizona

_____ 25. Arkansas

Telephone Etiquette, Time-Wasters, and Time Management Quiz

Directions: List *five* major rules under each of the four categories listed below.

Making Calls

Receiving Calls

Time Wasters

Time Management

Thinking Skills (Telephone) Quiz

Directions: Your employer, Mary Andrews, received the following messages during the week at times that she was out of the office. Write a paragraph for each message indicating what action you should take.

Message No. 1—January 23—from Sally Raf

Message No. 2—January 24—from Kwan Apiaah

Message No. 3—January 24—from Betty Hold

Message No. 4—January 24—from Jim Marks

Message No. 5—January 26—from Otto Ebermeyer

Message No. 6—January 25—from Newt Zimmer

Message No. 7—January 26—from Herman Holtzman

Message No. 8—January 27—from Millie Crane

For ___Mary___ **URGENT** ☐
Date ___Jan. 23___ Time ___2:10___

WHILE YOU WERE OUT

Mr/(Mrs)/Ms ___Sally Raf___
Of ___Union Bank___
Phone ___555-2390___ Ext. ___240___

☐ Phoned ☐ Please Call
☐ Stopped By ☐ Will Try Again
☐ Returned Call ☒ Wishes a Meeting

Message _____
___Would like a meeting to discuss a___
___seminar for the bank employees.___
___Would like to have it in May.___

___cd___

1

For ___Mary___ **URGENT** ☐
Date ___Jan. 24___ Time ___8:30___

WHILE YOU WERE OUT

(Mr)/Mrs/Ms ___Kwan Apiaah___
Of ___Western Co.___
Phone ___303-555-5491___ Ext. ___23___

☐ Phoned ☒ Please Call
☐ Stopped By ☐ Will Try Again
☐ Returned Call ☐ Wishes a Meeting

Message _____
___His company is having a special sale___
___on office products.___

___cd___

2

For ___Mary___ **URGENT** ☐
Date ___Jan. 24___ Time ___9:50___

WHILE YOU WERE OUT

Mr/(Mrs)/Ms ___Betty Hold___
Of ___Bismark and Andrews___
Phone ___813-555-9630___ Ext. ___92___

☐ Phoned ☐ Please Call
☐ Stopped By ☒ Will Try Again
☒ Returned Call ☐ Wishes a Meeting

Message _____
___I told her you were at a meeting and___
___would be in this p.m.___

___cd___

3

For ___Mary___ **URGENT** ☐
Date ___Jan. 24___ Time ___2:40___

WHILE YOU WERE OUT

(Mr)/Mrs/Ms ___Jim Marks___
Of ___Cleveland Supply___
Phone ___742-555-6248___ Ext. ___52___

☐ Phoned ☐ Please Call
☐ Stopped By ☐ Will Try Again
☐ Returned Call ☒ Wishes a Meeting

Message _____
___Wants to meet with you next week.___

___cd___

4

For ___Mary___   **URGENT** ☐
Date __Jan. 26__   Time __9:45__

WHILE YOU WERE OUT

Mr/Mrs/Ms __Otto Ebermeyer__
Of __Zack and Sons__
Phone __555-9332__   Ext. __45__

☐ Phoned   ☐ Please Call
☒ Stopped By   ☒ Will Try Again
☐ Returned Call ☐ Wishes a Meeting

Message
__Left some materials__

__cd__

5

For ___Mary___   **URGENT** ☐
Date __Jan. 25__   Time __10:30__

WHILE YOU WERE OUT

Mr/Mrs/Ms __Newt Zimmer__
Of __Omaha Technology__
Phone __555-2396__   Ext. __9__

☒ Phoned   ☒ Please Call
☐ Stopped By   ☐ Will Try Again
☐ Returned Call ☐ Wishes a Meeting

Message
__Has new equipment he wants to__
__show you. Wants a meeting next__
__week.__

__cd__

6

For ___Mary___   **URGENT** ☐
Date __Jan. 26__   Time __3:45__

WHILE YOU WERE OUT

(Mr)/Mrs/Ms __Herman Holtzman__
Of __Holtzman, Inc.__
Phone __555-9345__   Ext. __23__

☐ Phoned   ☐ Please Call
☐ Stopped By   ☐ Will Try Again
☐ Returned Call ☒ Wishes a Meeting

Message
__Needs to see you about a special__
__project he is working on.__

__cd__

7

For ___Mary___   **URGENT** ☐
Date __Jan. 27__   Time __11:30__

WHILE YOU WERE OUT

Mr/Mrs/(Ms) __Millie Crane__
Of __Millie's Creations__
Phone _____   Ext. ___

☒ Phoned   ☐ Please Call
☐ Stopped By   ☒ Will Try Again
☐ Returned Call ☐ Wishes a Meeting

Message

__cd__

8

Time Zone Differences Quiz

Directions: On the line at the left of the page, write the correct answer for each of the following items. You will need to refer to the *Company Procedures Manual* for the chart on time zone differences and to the map below for time zones.

_____   1.   If it is 5 p.m. in New York City, what time is it in Belgium?

_____   2.   If it is 2 a.m. in Denver, Colorado, what time is it in Sweden?

_____   3.   If it is 9 a.m. in Kansas City, Missouri, what time is it in Poland?

_____   4.   If it is noon in Dallas, Texas, what time is it in Mexico City?

_____   5.   If it is 10 p.m. in Los Angeles on May 5, what time is it in Ireland?

_____   6.   If it is 1 p.m. in Virginia, what time is it in Spain?

_____   7.   If it is 3 a.m. in Wyoming on June 10, what time is it in Japan?

_____   8.   If it is 8 a.m. in Iowa, what time is it in Germany?

_____   9.   If it is midnight in Reno, Nevada, what time is it in France?

_____   10.   If it is 4 p.m. in South Carolina on May 5, what time is it in Hong Kong?

_____   11.   If it is noon in New York City, what time is it in Los Angeles?

_____   12.   If it is 3 a.m. in Oregon, what time is it in Minnesota?

_____   13.   If it is midnight in Arkansas, what time is it in Georgia?

_____   14.   If it is 6 a.m. in West Virginia, what time is it in North Carolina?

_____   15.   If it is 10 a.m. in Arizona, what time is it in Oklahoma?

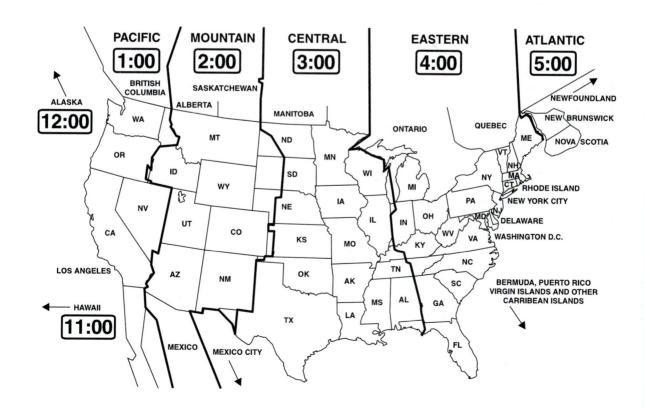

Word Usage Quiz

Directions: On the blank at the left of each sentence, place a C if it is correct and an I if it is incorrect.

_____   1. We were all right in the middle of a sound sleep when we were awakened by the crash.

_____   2. He will give her the best advice he can.

_____   3. She has already gone to the superintendent with the story.

_____   4. How will it affect her feelings for him?

_____   5. Her advise to her roommate was not very good.

_____   6. The kittens were all right next to the steps.

_____   7. We will except the money if he really owes it to us.

_____   8. It was almost noon when they arrived.

_____   9. We will accept the package if we know it is from him.

_____ 10. The argument was among Henry and Miriam.

_____ 11. We will chose sides for the basketball game.

_____ 12. Everyone will want to go once they hear about the prizes.

_____ 13. It is the forth time we have won the tournament.

_____ 14. Can you jump over that barrel?

_____ 15. She should divide the money between Mary, Bill, and Charles.

_____ 16. It's a good thing he didn't hear what she said.

_____ 17. The noon hour has passed, and we still haven't gone to lunch.

_____ 18. She went in the bedroom and had a good cry.

_____ 19. The Interstate goes from one coast to the other.

_____ 20. The latter solution is the best one.

_____ 21. We will proceed as planned.

_____ 22. There was quiet a rumpus on campus when they heard the news.

_____ 23. Their will be a lot of people at the party.

_____ 24. Will you call the role?

_____ 25. Is it too much to ask for you to come early and help?